The Idea of Community, Social Policy and Self

The Idea of Community, Social Policy and Self

Kevin Loughran

APJ Publications
Belfast

First published in 2003 by
APJ Publications
PO Box 526
Belfast, BT15 5YF
Northern Ireland

Printed in England by Antony Rowe Ltd
Chippenham, Wilts.

A CIP record for this book
is available from the British Library

ISBN 0 9543623 0 6

CONTENTS

Preface **ix**

Acknowledgements **x**

Introduction **1**

The Persistence of the Idea of Community – But Is There Such a Thing as Community?

Part I. The Idea of Community as an Element in Social Policy

1. Community and Informal Care **15**

What is community care?. – What and where is the community in community care?. – Community as the setting for the provision of services: in terms of being outside of institutions. – Community as the setting for the provision of services: in terms of locality, proximity and ordinariness. – Community as an agent for, or as a contributor to, the provision of services: as in informal care.

2. Health Care and Social Work Intervention **24**

Community as the end objective of helping activities: normalisation, rehabilitation and resettlement in the community (but which community?). – Community in terms of relating to other people. – Community as a process of interaction with other people in groups which is seen to advance health care or social work objectives. – Community as a process of self help and mutual support.

3. Area Regeneration Programmes **38**

The focus for area regeneration programmes – How are areas chosen? – Locality as a basis for area regeneration programmes – Assumptions about community in area regeneration programmes: about membership and cohesiveness

Part II. Is There Such a Thing as Community?

4. Is Human Nature Individual or Social? Is Community, Association or the State Artificial? **51**

Two different ways of looking at our social experience and our nature – the facts of existence: biology, genes and heredity – Does our biology make us individualistic?: genes and altruism – Co-operation and co-operative forms of association: how natural are they? – Do we begin on our own and learn to co-operate for our own advantage?

5. Locality and Community: Are Communities There? **88**

Is there an association between community and place? – Assumptions about community and place – Community, movement of people and change – Is there a link between community and place or community and space? – How important are definitions?

Part III. The Dimensions and the Limits of Community

6. Is There a Community Which Cares? **103**

Caring without community? – Caring and relationships – Caring, different kinds of help, and what people want for themselves – Conclusion: is there an association between community and caring?

7. Is the Idea of Community Realistic or Possible in Modern Economic and Social Conditions? **115**

Pessimistic perspectives: *Is the idea of community realistic today? – Is there a simple contrast between modern societies and older societies?*

Alternative perspectives: *Is the process of change in modern societies simple and straightforward? – Family and kin ties and social networks in modern society*

8. The Idea of Community and the Conflict of Values **132**

The idea of community as a value – Conflicts of values – Are conflicts of values inevitable? – Community as a value versus other values

9. The Multiplicity of Communities **138**

10. Does Everybody Want to Belong to a Community? **141**

11. Community, Belonging and Self **145**

Attachment, association and personal identity? – Who decides who a person is? – Being part of a community – Is there an individual self? – The social construction of self: at a simple level – The social construction of self: as a more complex process – The social construction of self: what it does not explain – The self and others: what is distinctive? – The self: do we start with nothing? Is it what we become or what we are predetermined? – The self: unique awareness and unique existence

Part IV. Conclusions

12. Unhelpful Applications of the Idea of Community **173**

Unitary community – The identification of community with physical space – Community and a thoroughly social sense of self – Community as a metaphor for other ideas

13. Helpful Applications of the Idea of Community **180**

As an idea of limited applicability – As representing common interests, interactions. association - As being dynamic

14. Two Ways in Which Social Policy May Make Use of the Idea of Community **184**

Community as a framework for relating to people – Community as a process of offering or giving support

APPENDICES

Appendix A **191**

What is Social Policy?

Appendix B **195**

Glossary of Chemical and Biological Terms as Used in Chapters 4 and 11

INDEX **203**

PREFACE

The Idea of Community, Social Policy and Self questions the idea of community. It questions many of the ways in which we use the word 'community' and the assumptions underlying those uses. It examines the idea of community in relation to community care, health care and social work interventions, and area regeneration programmes. It asks: 'Is community a useful idea to apply to our social experience? Is there such a thing as community?'

The book draws principally on case studies from the United Kingdom, including Northern Ireland, with some references to the Irish Republic. Laws, official reports and government departments which are referred to in the text are United Kingdom law, reports and departments unless stated otherwise. I would have liked to have used more case studies from, for example, North America, but it was a matter of practicality and convenience that I concentrate on material and situations with which I have some familiarity. Readers can judge for themselves to what degree this limitation affects the validity of my arguments, and the conclusions I reach.

The book draws on sources from English language countries and areas and refers in the main only to English language areas. Much of it consists of questioning of and conclusions arising from the various uses of that much used word 'community' and from ideas and ways of thinking which are expressed through it. I believe that it would be intellectually inadequate to assume that the various meanings of the English word 'community' and the various ideas and ways of thinking expressed through it are duplicated exactly in other-language countries and areas. I would suggest that examining the idea of community in relation to other-language countries and areas requires an additional study for each country or area. Each study would examine what variations there may be between the meaning of the word 'community' in English language usage and the meaning of similar words in the other language.

ACKNOWLEDGEMENTS

Some of the material for this book has its origins in my work for the degree of Master of Science in Social Policy, Planning and Administration at the University of Ulster. I would like to thank the university and in particular Professor John Offer for his advice and suggestions. I would also like to thank the staff at the University of Ulster Library, the Queen's University of Belfast Library, the Linenhall Library and Belfast Central Library for their help and advice. Thanks are due too to my brother Michael and my sister Anne for wordprocessing this work and for general help and advice. And last, but not least, thanks are due to Arthur Houston for his fine cover design.

Kevin Loughran *Belfast, November 2002*

The following have kindly given permission to reproduce copyright material:

The Isaiah Berlin Literary Trust for quotations from 'The Originality of Machiavelli', *Against the Current*, Oxford University Press (1981), first published by Hogarth (1979).

Oxford University Press and the Isaiah Berlin Literary Trust for a quotation from 'Two Concepts of Liberty', *Liberty*, edited by Henry Hardy, Oxford University Press (2002).

The Estate of Martin Buber for a quotation from *Between Man and Man*, translated by Ronald Gregor Smith, Routledge & Kegan Paul 1947).

Cambridge University Press for a quotation from Arthur Stanley Eddington, *New Pathways in Science* (1935).

The Estate of John Hewitt and The Irish Times (www.ireland.com) for a passage from an article which first appeared in The Irish Times of 4th July 1974.

Prof. Donald MacAulay for an extract from his poem 'Comharra Stiùridh', *Seòbhrach as a' Chlaich*, Gairm (1967).

Dr. Mary Midgley and Taylor & Francis for quotations from *The Ethical Primate*, Routledge (1994).

Prof. Philip Kitcher and Penguin for a quotation from *The Lives to Come,* Allen Lane, Penguin Press, © Andrew George Philip Kitcher (1996).

Penguin for a quotation from Erving Goffmann, *Asylums : Essays on the Social Situation of Mental Patients and other Inmates*, Penguin Press (1968), © Erving Goffmann (1961).

The Estate of Sir Karl Popper for a passage from *Unended Quest*, Routledge (1992), © Karl Popper 1974.

University of California Press / Journals for a passage from Barbara Katz Rothman, 'Of Maps and Imagination : Sociology Confronts the Genome', *Social Problems*, Vol.42, no.1 (February 1995), © The Society for the Study of Social Problems (1995).

Taylor and Francis for quotations from Ferdinand Tönnies, *Community and Association*, translated by Charles P. Loomis, Routledge & Kegan Paul (1995), first published 1955.

Taylor and Francis for a quotation from Raymond Plant, *Community and Ideology*, Routledge & Kegan Paul (1974).

Taylor and Francis for a quotation from Hilary Brown and Helen Smith, 'Normalisation : a Feminist Perspective', *Normalisation : a Reader for the Nineties*, edited by Hilary Brown and Helen Smith, Tavistock/Routledge (1992).

The Estate of Robert W Service for a passage from 'The Call of the Wild', *The Spell of the* Yukon, first published New York, Barse & Hopkins (1907).

The University of Chicago Press for quotations from Louis Wirth, 'Urbanism as a Way of Life', *American Journal of Sociology*, Vol.44, no.1 (1938).

Guardian Newspapers Ltd. for a quotation from David Cesarani, 'Between a rock and a hard place', *The Guardian* (21 September 1993). © Guardian 1993.

Guardian Newspapers Ltd. for quotations from Martin Woollacott, 'When brotherhood transcends borders', *The Guardian* (10th August 1994). © Guardian 1994.

INTRODUCTION

The persistence of the idea of community – but is there such a thing as community?

(1)

Few of us do not acknowledge the idea of community in some way or another, although often we acknowledge it by turning to the word 'community' as a habit of expression. For example, community is attached as a prefix to many titles of jobs or activities or institutions: community nurse, community social worker, community pharmacist, community policing, community workshops, community enterprises, community health centres; and so on.

The use of the word community carries assumptions, especially about relationships. To attach community to a job title is to imply that the workers who bear that title have different roles, and therefore different relationships with the people with whom they are working than other workers do who do not have community in their job titles. To attach community to the title of an institution, such as a school or a workshop or a health centre, is to imply that the staff who work in or administer the institution have different relationships with people who come to the institution to use it than staff who work elsewhere.

Often when we use the word community we are making assumptions about the reality of community in people's lives. The community is real. Communities are there. People belong to communities – irrespective of the actual state of their relationships. Even such an advocate for individualism as Robert Nozick – who in *Anarchy, State and Utopia* (1974) insisted that there were only different individual people leading their own individual lives [1] – referred repeatedly to community and communities, and assumed that we live in particular communities.[2] Community is a much older word and concept than is often recognised. the Oxford English Dictionary recognises seven different definitions or uses of the word. The most recent is traced to 1844; five are traced to the 17th century or earlier; and the oldest use is traced to 1375. The dictionary traces the definition of community as a body of people organised into a political, municipal or social unity and living in the same locality back to 1600.[3]

This variety of meanings helps to explain why community is such a persistent idea despite the problems of definition. It refers to our social experience: our relationships with each other in groups in all their complexity. And, as the Dictionary recognises, through most of its historical career community has been taken to refer both to a quality or state of existence and also to a body of individuals. Its use may express beliefs about the forms of association in which we engage with each other, about what is: and also aspirations about what ought to be.

(2)

The idea of community is a persistent and pervasive element in social policy statements and debates. Community may refer to where services are to be provided, as in 'care in the community'. It may refer to where particular centres from which services are organised and delivered are located – when they are described as being 'in the community' or in particular local communities. Community may be presented as a source of help and support for people who cannot function on their own; or as a process of self-help among groups of people supporting each other. Community, or local community, may be seen as the framework within which problems are experienced and solutions proposed or programmes of action introduced, whether these problems are defined as urban or rural poverty, or social exclusion, or economic change and decline. Community, or local communities, may be seen as agents for the implementation of aid programmes which have been initiated in areas by outside organisations to help address perceived problems of poverty or social exclusion or economic change, when those programmes of aid emphasise a need for ideas and participation and projects from 'the community'.

The idea of community may be considered as a means for assessing the impact on people of institutions or services or programmes of action, as in the demand that they be accountable 'to the community'. It may be considered as a means of assessing how decisions are taken and power is exercised, as in the demand that the community or local communities be consulted.

A notable example of the importance of the idea of community for the policies and the presentation of policies of public bodies is the 'Making Belfast Work' strategy statement of 1995. The 'Making Belfast Work' programme was launched originally by the Northern Ireland Government in 1988 to address the "economic, educational, health and environmental problems facing people who were living in the most disadvantaged areas of Belfast." [4] Within the sixteen pages of text the strategy statement of 1995 referred to 'the community', 'communities' or 'local communities' fifteen times. Communities were encouraged to become involved with government initiatives; government departments were urged to become accountable to communities and the wider community. The statement declared that the Making Belfast Work Programme was concerned with disadvantaged communities and that its purpose was to contribute to greater equity and increasing prosperity right across the community. The six Making Belfast Work area teams were to provide resources directly to communities. In addition to these references community was used frequently as a descriptive word as with community sector, community effort, community groups, community participation, community input.

Government departments and other bodies may appeal to the idea of community to justify particular policies and programmes. But the idea of community may be also a means for examining critically the impact on people of government policies and programmes, and of other factors. For example, Murray Hawtin, Geraint Hughes and Jaine Percy-Smith in *Community Profiling* (1994) discussed community profiles or social audits as tools for assessing the impact on people of economic change, or of changes in public policies and services, or of changes in the natural or social environment. The impact of these factors on people was to be seen and was to be studied as an impact on communities. Ideas about what to do were ideas about helping communities to respond.[5]

But although the idea of community is persistent and pervasive, often its relevance is assumed without it being discussed or tested. An outstanding example of this was the Seebohm Report (1968) on the personal social services in England and Wales which portrayed 'the community' as both the provider and the receiver of services.[6] The Barclay Report (1982) on the future of social work in England and Wales described community as networks of informal relationships between people. Again community was seen as a source of mutual support and assistance – although the report's authors admitted that no research had been carried out to gather evidence in relation to this or other statements in the report.[7]

Bruce Lynch and Richard Perry, in their review of case studies in community care in the United Kingdom (1992), referred to community being at the very heart of community care. But they admitted that although uses of the word might imply interpersonal interaction between people it could as well be used merely as a way of identifying a particular geographical locality – without any implication about the quality of relationships within that locality.[8]

Not only is the relevance of the idea of community assumed: often the reality of community – that it is there, that communities are real social units – is assumed. For example, Peter Barclay (1982) asserted that community is real – "We all know that it is there ..."[9]

This belief in the reality of community in people's lives is evident, as suggested above, in the assumption that people belong to particular communities irrespective of the actual state of their relationships. Eric Emerson and Chris Hatton (1994), in reviewing research on the relocation from hospital to community of people with learning disabilities, acknowledged that isolation was a common experience of former hospital residents. They referred to former residents' "lack of real presence in their communities."[10] But if they lacked real presence, then why refer to 'their' communities?

Although assumptions about the relevance of the idea of community and the reality of community in people's lives may be commonplace, community remains a contested idea. It is contested as to whether community exists or can be defined or whether the idea of community is of any practical value. For example, Martin Bulmer (1987) complained that attempts to clarify what community meant became self-defeating. [11] Robert Pinker (1982) argued that the 'intangible' idea of community could not provide a basis for equitable and rational social policies. [12]

Community is also a contested idea as to whether it represents a positive experience or a positive value. Some feminists have reacted to the idea of community in social policy with scepticism and hostility, seeing it as a means for shifting responsibility for support of people in need to women, unpaid. Elizabeth Wilson (1982) argued that often when the term community was used in connection with welfare provision, what was meant was family; and not only family, but women. [13] Gillian Dalley (1992) identified care in the community with an emphasis on living lives in relative isolation in small units dependent on a limited range of other people.[14]

Some feminists may react against the idea of community or the particular way in which it is used because it seems to promise something more and different from what many women experience who are confined to a private sphere by the demands of supporting a frail partner or parent or relative. But some people may reject community itself as a value. Albert Hunt and Stephnie Rigel (1986) argued that a cohesive, mutually interdependent sense of community might not be the ultimate value for everyone. [15] Community, association, a collective sense of identity may not be what some people want for themselves, either at particular stages of their lives or for their lives in general. Some people prefer to 'keep themselves to themselves.' So there is at least a possibility of conflict between individual aspirations and personal values on the one side, and the requirements of association and group loyalty on the other side.

(3)

To explore the idea of community, I examine in Part 1 meanings which are attached to the word community in selected areas of policy and practice: in community care; in health care and social work intervention; and in area regeneration programmes, whether these programmes are directed at poverty or social exclusion or unemployment or economic decline.

But is there such a thing as community? Is it an appropriate or useful idea to apply to our social experience? If (to quote Robert Nozick's phrase) there are only different individual people leading their own individual lives, it can be argued that each person learns to co-operate with other people merely as the necessary means to self-protection and self-advancement. And the different forms of association between people, from small and informal to large-scale and formal, are no more than arrangements which are necessary in order to protect or advance our various individual interests.

If human nature is essentially individualist, in the sense that all human behaviour is motivated ultimately by self-interest, then can the idea of community have any validity as a means of describing our relationships with other people? Straightforward words such as 'association' or 'group' or 'grouping' would be preferable: words which refer simply to people coming together for some common purpose but do not in themselves imply any quality of relationship.

But if the groups and associations in which we are involved with other people are part of what and who we are, if co-operation is a fundamental fact of our existence and our being, then it will not be sufficient to interpret our social experience in terms of the arrangements which individual people make with each other. It will be necessary to consider the quality of our relationships.

So to explore the idea of community further, I consider in Part 2 why and how people associate with each other in groups and ask: are relationships with other people simply means to individual ends; or are they ends in themselves? If relationships with other people are ends in themselves then the idea of community can have some validity as a means of describing what is common between people, as distinct from simpler words such as 'association' or 'group' or 'grouping'.

If the idea of community has some validity as a means of describing what is common between people, perhaps community can be expressed as actual social units. This is implied, for example, in Robert Nozick's assertion that we all live in particular communities. It is implied in the association between community and place, when we talk about 'local communities.' So when considering the reality of community, in asking if there is such a thing as community, I examine in Part 2 the association between community and place and ask: are communities there?

(4)

If association with other people can be a reflection of our real needs and nature, then the idea of community may be a valid idea to apply to our social experience; but if it is, how far can it go? What are the limits of community?

Perhaps community is a less important dimension of our social experience than we believe. There is much that the idea of community does not explain, to which the idea of community is not relevant. Perhaps the idea of community is not realistic in the modern world. And perhaps community is not always a good idea. So in Part 3 I explore the dimensions and the limits of community.

Firstly, in view of the emphasis on the idea of community in present social policy debates, to which I have referred above, I ask in Chapter 6: is there a community which cares? Who gives personal help to people who need it, and in what circumstances and on what terms? There is substantial evidence to indicate that often giving personal help to individual people in need is personal, private and isolating for those people giving the help. However, the argument that this kind of evidence proves that there is no 'community which cares' is too simple. It does not take account of the wishes of the people who need and receive help: their sense of privacy and from whom they wish to receive help. Therefore in this chapter I examine different helping relationships and what they indicate about limits to the relevance of the idea of community.

In Chapter 7 I explore the belief that the idea of community is neither realistic nor possible in modern economic and social conditions: that the growth of modern cities, local and international market pressures and increased personal mobility are pushing people further apart and are promoting relations based on calculations of self-interest. Modern industrial society, it is supposed, is undermining personal relationships and forms of association between groups of people which are based on personal relationships. I argue that these beliefs and suppositions may arise from an exaggeration of the significance of community and consequently an exaggeration of the supposed decline of community compared to past times.

In Chapter 8 I consider community as representing a value: as a sense of what people believe to be good or bad, desirable or undesirable about their involvement with other people in various forms of association. I explore issues which are not considered very often in relation to the idea of community: that community can be seen as a value, but that there are other values which may conflict at certain times with community as a value; that at certain times, in certain situations the idea of community or particular expressions of it may appear – to some people – to be of negative value. It may not be possible ever to eliminate entirely conflicts of values. So it follows that in certain situations where the value of community is seen by some people as being in conflict with other values which they hold to be more important, then those people should reject the value of community.

In Chapter 9 I explore the idea that each of us in our lives will relate to or participate in a variety of forms of association. If we may use the word community here, we can say that each of us will experience a multiplicity of communities with various degrees of belonging at different stages of our lives. They may represent different aspects of our relationships with each other at different stages of our lives.

Ideas of involvement and belonging lead to the next question, which I discuss in Chapter 10. This is: does everybody want to belong to a community – in general, or at particular times in particular situations? It is difficult to avoid the conclusion that some people, at certain times in certain situations do not want to 'belong to a community.'

This discussion leads to the final questions about the dimensions and the limits of community, which I consider in Chapter 11: to what degree can we discuss individual persons' relationships with other people in terms of the forms of association in which they are involved? To what degree can we identify individual persons with the forms of association in which they are involved, to which they could be said to belong? To what degree – if at all – can we identify self with community?

(5)

Community is a persistent idea despite the problems of defining it, because it refers to our social experience: our relations with each other in groups in all their complexity. So in offering some conclusions about the idea of community, I prefer to examine different applications of the idea of community rather than attempt yet another definition.

The assumption that the problems or issues presented by an idea (such as the idea of community) can be resolved only by defining the terms used (for example, by defining community) ignores the difficulties involved in trying to define any terms exactly or uniformly. Karl Popper (1945) complained that the importance of the meaning of terms had been exaggerated : he believed that the precision of a language depended upon not demanding that its terms be precise.[16]

For Karl Popper this principle would have applied especially to the process of scientific enquiry. John Scales and Roel Snieder dealt with this problem of defining terms used in scientific enquiry in their article 'What is a Wave?' (*Nature* (1999).[17] Waves are present everywhere in nature. They are central to the structure of matter and time and to many physical, biological and chemical phenomena. But the puzzle persists: what is a wave? John Scales and Roel Snieder admitted that even people whose job is to work with, to study and to understand the variety of waves in nature are prone to confusion and vagueness when confronted with this question. However, this confusion and difficulty in arriving at a uniform definition of waves does not prevent the process of understanding waves and wave phenomena, or prevent practical applications of that understanding. (In their article, John Scales and Roel Snieder presented a wave as a disturbance or imbalance in the forces that connect 'bits of matter' together. What makes a wave distinctive is that this is not a single disturbance: it is disturbance which propagates. So they offered a definition of a wave as an organised propagating imbalance – but they pleaded with readers not to ask them to define 'organised'!)

So in examining different applications of the idea of community I examine firstly applications which I consider are unhelpful because they do not correspond with the reality of our social experience. These applications are: the presumption of a unitary community or unitary communities; the identification of community with physical space; the idea of community based on a thoroughly social sense of self; and community as a link to and as a metaphor for other ideas such as consultation, accountability and participation.

Then I present applications of the idea of community which I consider are helpful because they correspond with the reality of our social experience. These applications are: community as an idea of limited applicability; community as representing common interests, interaction and association; and community as being dynamic.

Finally, I propose two ways in which I believe social policy, as programmes of intervention by agencies or organised groups, or as deliberate helping activities by particular people, may make use realistically of the idea of community.

REFERENCES

1. NOZICK, Robert. (1974). *Anarchy, state and utopia.* Oxford: Blackwell. p.33
2. *ibid.* pp.304-332
3. *OXFORD English Dictionary.* (1978 repr.). Oxford: Clarendon
4. MAKING Belfast Work. (1985). *Strategy statement.* Belfast: HMSO
5. HAWTIN, Murray, HUGHES, Geraint, and PERCY-SMITH, Jaine. (1994). *Community profiling : auditing social needs.* Buckingham: Open University Press. pp.4-5
6. *REPORT of the Committee on Local Authority and Allied Personal Services* [Seebohm Report]. (1968). London: HMSO. para. 475
7. BARCLAY Committee. (1982). *Social workers : their roles and tasks.* London: Bedford Square Press. para. 13-24

8. LYNCH, Bruce, and PERRY, Richard. (1992). New worlds in community care, *Experiences of community care : case studies of UK practice.* Harlow: Longman. p.2

9. BARCLAY, Peter. (1982). The report and its implications, *A new direction for social work?.* Edited by Terry Philpott. Sutton: Community Care/IPC. p.8

10. EMERSON, Eric, and HATTON, Chris. (1994). *Moving out : relocation from hospital to community.* London: HMSO. Introduction, p.iii

11. BULMER, Martin. (1987). *The social basis of community care.* London: Unwin Hyman. p.35

12. PINKER, Robert. (1982). Family services, *Challenges to social policy.* Edited by R. Berthoud. Aldershot: Gower/PSI. p.15

13. WILSON, Elizabeth. (1982). Women, community and family, *The family, state and social policy.* Edited by Alan Walker. Oxford: Basil Blackwell & Martin Robertson. p.40

14. DALLEY, Gillian. (1992). Social welfare ideologies and normalisation, *Normalisation : a reader for the Nineties.* Edited by Hilary Brown and Helen Smith. London: Tavistock/Routledge. p.106

15. HUNT, Albert, and RIGEL, Stephnie. (1986). The meaning of community in community mental health, *Journal of Community Psychology* (Rutland, VT: Clinical Psychology Publishing Co.). Vol.14, no.1 (January 1986)

16. POPPER, Karl. (1945, repr. 1975). *The open society and its enemies.* Vol.2. London: Routledge & Kegan Paul. p19

17. SCALES, John, and SNIEDER, Roel. (1999). What is a wave? *Nature* (London: Macmillan Magazines), Vol.401 (21 October 1999)

Part 1

The Idea of Community as an Element in Social Policy

1

COMMUNITY CARE AND INFORMAL CARE

What is community care? – What and where is the community in community care? – Community as the setting for the provision of services: in terms of being outside of institutions – Community as the setting for the provision of services: in terms of locality, proximity, and ordinariness – Community as the agent for or the contributor to the provision of services: as in 'informal care' – Community as an agent for or as a contributor to the provision of services: as in informal care

What is community care?

In 1990 the Department of Health in London, in giving guidance on the National Health Service and Community Care Act, defined community care as "...the provision of services and support which people who are afflicted by problems of ageing, mental illness, mental handicaps, physical or sensory disability need to be able to live as independently as possible in their homes or in 'homely' settings in their community..." [1]

Care in the community as a form of supporting people with long term needs is not new. The Personal Social Services Research Unit (1992) argued that a loose system of services delivered to people outside of hospitals had been a feature of British health and welfare policy at least since the 18th century. [2]

Gillian Parker (1991) saw community care first emerging as a recognisable concept in UK government policy at the beginning of the 20th century, in relation to guardianship and supervision orders for people with a mental handicap.[3] Alan Walker (1982) identified the first use of the term as being in 1957 in the 'Report of the Royal Commission on the Law Relating to Mental Illness' which talked of moving people from hospital care to community care.[4]

Gillian Parker claimed that there was general agreement on the assumptions underlying community care: they refer to people moving out of institutions. But she acknowledged that community care may mean different things to different people.[5] The House of Commons Social Services Committee (1985) complained that "... community care ... has in fact come to have such general reference as to be virtually meaningless. It has become a slogan." [6]

What and where is the community in community care?

Community, asserted Bruce Lynch and Richard Perry (1992), is at the very heart of community care.[7] Usually however, it is not explained what is meant by the community in community care. Most often it appears as being a state of being different from something else, *e.g.* of being outside of hospitals and large institutions. The PSSRU (Personal Social Services Research Unit), in reviewing the Care in the Community Demonstration Programme on behalf of the Department of Health studied a number of pilot projects (1992). It found *de facto* definitions of community which ranged from independent living to residential homes : almost any accommodation besides hospitals.[8] It should be noted that the policy guidance issued by the Department of Health in 1990, which is quoted above, sought to define community care but offered no definition of community and no explanation of what it meant by the term.

Robbie Gilligan (1991) noted the contradictions in the Irish Republic between what was included under the heading of community care and what was not, and what community referred to and what it did not. Under the 1970 Health Act, health services in the Irish Republic were reorganised under eight regional boards. Services within each board were divided into a number of programmes, each with its own manager. The community care programme, which ranged from GP and home nursing services to personal social services and support for voluntary organisations, and to health promotion and education, included also some institutional services, *e.g.* children's homes. It excluded some non-institutional services which were "based in the community" and had a "major domiciliary extension to their work", *e.g.* mental handicap and child guidance services.[9]

There are, it seems to me, two main ways in which 'community' as an idea (or simply as an 'add-on' word) is used in relation to the range of services and helping activities which may be brought under the heading of community care. Firstly, community is seen as a setting for the provision of services, usually by government bodies or charitable organisations. Secondly, community is seen as an agent for or contributor to the provision of services as in 'informal care'.

Community as the setting for the provision of services : in terms of being outside of institutions

In 1959, the Minister of Health, speaking in the House of Commons on the new Mental Health Act, stated that one of the main principles underlying the Act was the re-orientation of mental health services away from institutional care towards care in the community.[10] In 1985 the Audit Commission identified a trend in the previous one hundred years away from accommodating the most disabled members of society in institutions, many of which were "large, remote and impersonal"; and a trend towards supporting people "in the community where they and their families have lived." [11] In 1988, the Griffiths Report discussed community care in terms of shifting the balance of helping services from hospitals to the community.[12] In 1993 the Department of Health and Social Services in Northern Ireland, in a leaflet aimed at the general public, described community care as meaning care given outside hospital and consisting of both health and social care. [13]

But if community care means movement from hospitals and institutions, there is some confusion as to what community care means in terms of movement to. David Hunter and Gerard Wistow (1987) pointed out how different organisations and services may have quite different perspectives on this question. Traditionally for health services, community care has meant shifting the centre of gravity from hospital to predominantly local government residential services, whereas for social services community care has meant shifting the centre of gravity from residential to domiciliary or day care services.[14] The

Griffiths Report considered the full range of community care services to include services provided to people in their own homes, in group homes, in residential care units and in nursing homes.[15]

Identifying care in the community with such a range of supported or managed accommodation, other than people's own personal dwellings, raises the question: what is or should be the dividing line between institutional and non-institutional care? Gillian Parker (1990) has claimed "general agreement" on the benefits of dependent people living outside of "large, segregated institutions." [16] But if segregation / integration and size are to be the basis for deciding whether or not helping services can be classified as institutional or non-institutional, further questions arise. Where is the dividing line between to be drawn between negative segregation from the community and positive integration in and with the community? When does negative large size become positive small size?

Hilary Brown and Helen Smith (1992), in their discussion of small group homes, pointed to two types of segregation "... large numbers of people in a large communal building off the bus route behind walls ... and in ones and twos in private spaces." [17] John L. McKnight (1992) during his visit to a group home in an 'ordinary' house in and 'ordinary' street in a small New England town, found that the residents – four middle-aged men – had almost no social relationships with neighbours or townspeople. He demanded that services should not be called community services if they did not involve people in what he called community relationships. [18]

It is not physical size or location but access, relationships and autonomy which are important in determining opportunities for people to participate in social life.

Community as the setting for the provision of services : in terms of locality, proximity and ordinariness

The Griffiths Report (1988) sought to place responsibility for care for people who need support with the local community and as near as possible to the individual needing support, and his/her carer.[19]

The idea of local community in the development of community care services was promoted by the Department of Health and Social Services Inspectorate (1991) in their advice on training for managers. Their declared purpose was to help managers prepare for partnerships with 'local communities'.[20]

The House of Commons Social Services Committee (1985) emphasised nearness and ordinariness as basic elements of community care. It offered general principles for a definition of community care which included a preference for local services over distant services, and an emphasis on enabling individuals to live as normal a life as possible.[21]

But it is too easy to assume that living in a particular setting or in a particular location in themselves involves people 'in the community' or in the community that is presumed to exist at a certain place or among the people who are resident within that place. In effect what such an assumption does is to equate institutional setting or type of residence, or physical location, with personal or social relationships. It is assumed that relationships will develop because of and on the basis of type of residence and physical location.

An example of this way of discussing community was provided by Felix Lynch's report on the development of the Trinity Centre in Edinburgh which was set up for people who had severe disabilities (1992). Although the centre had been located 'in the community' for thirteen years, there had been little real contact between the disabled users of the centre and the people living around and near it. (Eventually contact and relationships did develop between the two).[22]

Another example of this use of the idea of community, when there is in effect an absence of relationships, has been noted above in John L. McKnight's account of his visit to a small New England town. He was moved to demand that services should not be described as 'community services' when there was an absence of 'community relationships.'

Nearness and physical location will not in themselves make relationships, although they may facilitate the development of relationships. An example has been the establishment in

Manchester of Gandhi Hall, a day centre for elderly Indian people, especially those living on their own. Mr. Mamitora and Doctor Daz (1992) described the scepticism of the Director of Social Services when presented with the proposal for what he saw as a separate, specialised centre. He said that elderly Indian people were welcome to use the local day centre operated by his department. Mr. Mamitora and Doctor Daz argued that elderly Indian people couldn't go there: they didn't understand English, and there were differences in diet, religion and culture.

The Gandhi Centre was so successful that it began to take people from further afield, from the Greater Manchester area, because there were no other day centres for older Indian People.[23] Nearness or physical location did not help the Ghandi Centre's development: familiarity, identification with the centre and realistic opportunities for communication did.

Community as an agent for, or as a contributor to the provision of services as in 'informal care'

The Seebohm Report on Personal Social Services in England and Wales (1968) offered a broad and optimistic view of the community as the provider of services as well as the recipient of services. [24] The Barclay Report on the Future of Social Work (1982) took a rather more specific but still optimistic view of care in the community as a network or networks of informal relationships between people who were connected with each other. It perceived an important feature of community to be the capacity of networks of people within it to mobilise individual and collective responses to adversity; and it asserted that the bulk of social care within England and Wales was provided by ordinary people acting individually or as members of spontaneously formed groups.[25]

At the same time policy makers have put more emphasis on the community as a personal, informal and partly individual thing. The Department of Health (1990) considered that most support for vulnerable people is provided by families, friends and neighbours. [26] In Northern Ireland the 1990 White Paper

People First accepted that the great bulk of community care is provided by family, friends and neighbours.[27]

Care by people outside the framework of statutory and voluntary agencies and professional roles has been described as 'informal care' (for example, Rosanne Cecil, John Offer and Fred St. Leger (1987) [28]). But how much do the relationships, networks and activities which are described justify the use of the term community? 'Community', I would suggest, implies some degree or form of common bond. It implies public and social as compared to private and personal. Community care as it is presented often could be taken to imply some of these suggested elements of community in relation to activities for the support and care of dependent people. Informal care, as a aspect of community care, could be taken to imply some of these same elements of community.

However, Anna Briggs and Judith Oliver (1985), in their compilation of the experiences and views of carers, reported that carers were sick of hearing about community care which often, as far as they were concerned, meant themselves single-handed.[29]

So what and where is the community which cares? There is a considerable body of research which suggests that it is not there; that assistance for dependent people, other than when it is provided by statutory and voluntary agencies and professional workers, is essentially personal and often private and even isolating. The research indicates that assistance is provided most often by family members and other kin rather than by neighbours or friends; and that even then it is provided most often by one principal carer who is usually a woman. The evidence from this research is examined in Part 3: Chapter 6.

But in itself this conclusion – that assistance for dependent people is mainly personal, private and isolating – does not take full account of the complexity of relationships which may develop between people within family and kin ties and beyond family and kin ties. It is unreasonable to assert that there is a community waiting out there ready to provide assistance before examining evidence. Equally, it is unreasonable to assert that there is no community or such a thing as community which provides or offers assistance before examining evidence. Again I seek to do this in Part 3: Chapter 6.

REFERENCES

1. HEALTH, Department of. (1990). *Community care in the next decade and beyond : policy guidance.* London: HMSO. Appendix B2
2. PERSONAL SOCIAL SERVICES Research Unit. (1992). *Care in the community : challenge and demonstration.* Aldershot: Ashgate. p.3
3. PARKER, Gillian. (1990). *With due care and attention.* London: Family Policy Studies Centre. p.7
4. WALKER, Alan. (1982). The meaning and social division of community care, *The family, state and social policy.* Edited by Alan Walker. Oxford: Basil Blackwell & Martin Robertson. p.15
5. PARKER, Gillian. (1990). *With due care and attention.* pp.7-8
6. HOUSE OF COMMONS, Social Services Committee. (1985). *Report on community care : with special reference to adult mentally ill and mentally handicapped people.* London: HMSO. para. 8
7. LYNCH, Bruce, and PERRY, Richard. (1992). *Experiences of community care : case studies in UK practice.* Harlow: Longman. p.2
8. PERSONAL SOCIAL SERVICES Research Unit. (1992). *Care in the community : challenge and demonstration.* p.6
9. GILLIGAN, Robbie. (1991). *Irish child care services.* Dublin: Institute of Public Administration. pp.95-96
10. WALKER, Alan. (1982). The meaning and social division of community care, *The family, state and social policy.* p.15
11. AUDIT COMMISSION for England and Wales. (1986). *Making a reality of community care.* London: HMSO. para. 2
12. GRIFFITHS, Roy (Chairman). (1988). *Community care : agenda for action.* London: HMSO. paras. 3.6 & 4.13
13. HEALTH AND SOCIAL SERVICES, Department of (Northern Ireland). (1993). *Community care changes from April 1993*
14. HUNTER, David, and WISTOW, Gerard. (1987). *Community care in Great Britain : variations on a theme.* London: King Edward Fund. p.87

15. GRIFFITHS, Roy (Chairman). (1988). *Community care : agenda for action.* para. 2.6

16. PARKER, Gillian. (1990). *With due care and attention.* p.8

17. BROWN, Hilary, and SMITH, Helen. (1992). Normalisation : a feminist perspective, *Normalisation : a reader for the Nineties.* Edited by Hilary Brown and Helen Smith. London: Tavistock/Routledge. p.153

18. McKNIGHT, John L. (1992). Redefining community, *Social Policy* (New York: Social Policy Corporation). Vol.23, no.2 (Fall-Winter). pp.56-62

19. GRIFFITHS, Roy (Chairman). (1988). *Community care : agenda for action.* Intro., para. 30

20. HEALTH, Department of, Social Services Inspectorate. (1991). *Training for community care : a joint approach.* London: HMSO. para. 3.13

21. HOUSE OF COMMONS, Social Services Committee. (1985). *Report on community care.* paras. 10-11

22. LYNCH, Felix. (1992). The community garden, *Experiences of community care : case studies of UK practice.* Edited by Bruce Lynch and Richard Perry. Harlow: Longman. p.14

23. DAZ, Dr., and MAMITORA, Mr. (1992). The Gandhi Hall Day Centre, *Experiences of community care : case studies of UK practice.* p.41

24. REPORT of the Committee on Local Authority and Allied Personal Social Services (Seebohm Report). (1968). London: HMSO. para. 475

25. BARCLAY Committee. (1982). *Social workers : their roles and tasks.* London: Bedford Square Press. para. 13.24

26. HEALTH, Department of. (1990). *Community care in the next decade and beyond.* London: HMSO. para. 3.207

27. HEALTH AND SOCIAL SERVICES, Department of (Northern Ireland). (1990). *People first.* Belfast: HMSO. p.5

28. CECIL, Rosanne, OFFER, John, and ST. LEGER, Fred. (1987). *Informal welfare.* Aldershot: Gower. pp.4-5

29. BRIGGS, Anna, and OLIVER, Judith. (1985). *Caring : experiences of looking after disabled relatives.* London: Routledge & Kegan Paul. Intro., p.xviii

2

HEALTH CARE AND SOCIAL WORK INTERVENTION

Community as an end objective of helping activity : normalisation, rehabilitation, resettlement 'in the community' – Which community?– Community in terms of relating to others (or not) – Community as a process of self-help and mutual support

Community as an end objective of helping activity : normalisation, rehabilitation, resettlement in the 'community'

The promotion of 'community care' as a strategy for health and social services has meant that relocation from hospitals and institutions into the 'community' has been a major concern for health care and social work staff. From the 1959 Mental Health Act through the 1963 and 1969 Children and Young Persons Acts, legislation in Britain has stressed the desirability of avoiding institutional care. Between 1983 and 1993 the number of places in local government homes in England and Wales declined from 116,400 to 68,900; and the number of National Health Service beds for geriatric patients declined from 56,000 to 38,000. Between 1976 and 1996 the number of beds available for admissions on the grounds of mental health declined from 97,000 to 55,000.[1]

However, usually what the community is which is supposed to be the end objective of relocation programmes is not explained or defined. Some health care and social work staff interpret it very much in terms of the greater personal autonomy and personal choice which alternative forms of living are seen to offer in comparison with hospitals and large institutions. This was a central concern of the Kirklees Relocation Project, which was reviewed by Tim Booth, Ken Simon and Wendy Booth (1990). They considered the project to be largely successful on its own terms.[2] They interviewed forty-five people in the care of local authorities who had moved from hospitals to hostels.

Some had moved further, from hostels to independent living accommodation. They interviewed the people before they moved out of hospital, shortly after they moved out and again one year afterwards. One year afterwards the overwhelming majority of those who had moved remained positive about the move. Tim Booth, Ken Simon and Wendy Booth concluded that the policy of relocating people from hospital and developing 'community alternatives' was entirely in keeping with the wishes of the people themselves.

Some people emphasise integration with the community and ordinariness as objectives for relocation. The idea of ordinariness is central to the philosophy of normalisation. For Linda Ward (1991), ordinariness for people with severe learning difficulties meant access to houses, jobs, workplaces, friends, neighbours and social and leisure activities to enable them to live in the community like everyone else.[3]

But the idea of ordinariness, of integration in the community which is the concern of normalisation, is problematic. Gillian Dalley (1992) complained that the essence of normalisation seemed to be conformity.[4] Eric Emerson (1992) pointed out that if equality was being sought for people with learning difficulties, equality did not necessarily require integration.[5]

The idea of integration in the community is problematic because it does not take account of the complexity of relationships. Sue Szivas (1992) complained that advocates of normalisation had overlooked some basic psychological processes. She referred to studies which indicated that perceiving yourself as being stigmatised correlated with perceiving yourself as being inferior to persons with whom you compared yourself. People with learning difficulties who were in integrated settings might compare themselves with people to whom they felt inferior.[6] Normalisation, complained Sue Szivas, persisted in denying difference or in viewing it negatively. She supported the promotion of separate group identities. But this did not mean support for a return to segregation.

Relocation from hospital to the community can bring benefits for the people who are moving out, but it is not in itself equivalent to relationships. Eric Emerson and Chris Hatton

(1994) reviewed research in the United Kingdom on the impact of relocation on the lives of people with learning difficulties. They found that people moving out from hospitals might expect certain benefits in terms of more choice, more opportunities for exercising skills, more access and more acceptance. But there was little evidence that these users of community based services were developing new competencies or new relationships: they had few relationships with non-disabled people.[7]

Which community?

I have argued above that the idea of integration with the community is problematic because it does not take account of the complexity of relationships. It is problematic also because the idea of community itself is problematic. The idea of relocation into the community and integration with the community makes 'the community' the end objective of helping activity. But is it one community, or more than one? Are people who are moving out of hospital or large institutions being helped to relocate in the same community? Is everyone who is being helped to integrate with the community being helped to integrate with the same community?

It would be more appropriate, I believe, to consider that people who are moving out of hospitals or large institutions are seeking to or are hoping to make connections with different communities; rather than 'the community'. So it would be appropriate to ask: what and where is the community of community care; or the communities of particular community care projects? Different projects, different situations, different people may mean different communities, as the cases described below illustrate.

Gandhi Hall in Manchester (see Chapt. 1, p.20) was an example of a day centre established for a particular group of people: in this case, older Indian people. To talk about a centre as being in the community or as being nearby, was neither sufficient nor appropriate, the founders of the centre believed. What older Indian people needed was a centre which reflected their community, in terms of their language, their diet, their religion and their culture. Neither the precise location of the centre nor its geographical catchment area were as important as familiarity, identification with the institution and realistic opportunities to communicate with other people.

Another example of the importance of cultural or personal identification rather than physical location in facilitating opportunities for communication and self-expression was provided by the Handsworth Community Care Centre in Birmingham. The centre was founded in 1983 to cater largely – but not exclusively – for Afro-Caribbean people with mental health problems who had been in trouble with the law. When they were asked what they wanted, they said a centre which would cater for the food, mainly Afro-Caribbean, which they ate; a centre in which they could talk loudly, express their own ideas and feel safe.[8]

The community in a community care project may develop when people recognise common problems and concerns and share them and work together for solutions. Shula Allan and B. Morris (1992) described the Oasis project which was supported by the Edinburgh Association for Mental Health. It was a self-help group for 'local' women which worked very much through the women supporting each other by sharing their experiences and problems. The group developed a home visiting service which was co-ordinated by the group members.[9] The community in this community care project was not the 'local community' or the places of residence of the women in the group. Rather it was the women themselves as a group, acknowledging common problems and interests and working together on them.

And do people want the same things for themselves in terms of community and relationships with others? Paul Simic (1994) reported on a mental health relocation project in Edinburgh. Between November 1989 and December 1990 he interviewed twenty-four younger adults who had experienced major psychiatric disorders and who had been patients at the Royal Edinburgh Hospital. Most of them were seen as 'revolving door' patients who had been in and out of hospital. In most cases they moved out to supported accommodation. Paul Simic found that the number of them with close alliances involving a number of people was small and only six had 'reasonably extensive' networks. But their expectations and what they wanted for themselves were not identical. Some would have wanted better relationships but some definitely did not want that kind of intimacy. [10]

Different people in the same situation may make quite different assessments of where they are and where they want to be. Jenny Morris, in her study of community and disabled people (1993) observed quite different attitudes to residential care as alternatively limiting freedom and extending freedom. Some people felt they were made dependent by residential care but other people felt that it gave them a freedom which they could not have in their parents' home (although many people commented on a lack of privacy in residential care and a lack of control over the procedures of residential life).[11]

Community in terms of relating to others (or not)

John L. McKnight (1992) described a visit to a group home in a small New England town in a state where very few people were resident in large institutions, and small group homes had proliferated. The particular group home he visited was in a house indistinguishable from others in the street. It was home to five middle-aged men, one of whom had lived there for ten years.

John McKnight was invited to appreciate how the residents of the home were part of the community. But when he enquired with them about their lives, their experiences and their relationships in the town, he found that they had almost no social relationships with neighbours or townspeople; that none could identify a close local friend or neighbour; and that none were involved in any kind of organisation, association or club. [12]

It could be said that at the core of this failure to achieve the objective of integration with the community was the failure or non-development of social relationships (which I define as relationships with a variety of people beyond close family and kin ties which are entered into or sustained according to the person's own choice). Relationships have been central to the difficulties of normalisation as discussed above.

But as well as the failure and non-development of relationships there have been successes. For example, Alan Tyne (1992), reporting on case studies of success in integration, described the case of Susan, who had lived in an institutional world for women who had been and were violent; but who was helped over time to settle successfully in her own flat and make her own life – 'in the community', if you like. No doubt Susan benefited from the skilled professional support she received, but it was evident that the development of positive relationships – relationships which she entered into according to her choice – was central to the success of her resettlement: and central to those relationships was the discovery that she could make a contribution to the lives of people around her.[13]

Relationships can be crucial both to the obstacles and to the opportunities presented to a person in his or her life. Jonathan Griffiths, in a special supplement to *Community Care* magazine (1978), described his life with a disability from childhood to eventual success in independent living and in a career. He described the variety of factors which restricted his life and affected his confidence in trying to shape it according to his terms: family prejudice, social prejudice, physical environment and economic circumstances.

In his childhood, integration was easy: other children were accepting. In his late teens and early adulthood things changed for the worse as his social and cultural environment changed. Prospects improved with the acquisition of his first personal motorised transport, but this led to further strains in his relationship with his mother – up to then his mother had been the instigator of his life's achievements.

A crucial factor in Jonathan Griffiths' life was his involvement with local Quaker groups where he enjoyed both acceptance on equal terms and support. He emphasised especially the two-way relationships which he developed with older members.

He decided eventually that he must leave home and set up his own household. This caused further strain in his relationship with his mother. It prompted also a year long battle with Social

Security before finally he was paid benefit. His independent status and his integration 'with the community' – as himself, on his own terms – was underwritten finally by his achieving success as a computer programmer.[14]

In Jonathan Griffiths' case, and in other similar cases, 'community' may be taken as metaphor for that whole area of relationships with other people outside of family entered into, in the main, by oneself.

'Community' as a process of interaction with other people in groups, which is seen to advance health care or social work objectives

Working with people in groups is an established method in health care and social work practice. But a distinction can be made between different forms of group work practice on the basis of what the group process is for and what the worker's role is. A distinction can be made between bringing people together in a group as a means of helping individual members of the group work through personal problems, and bringing people together – or helping people to come together – in a group when promoting the process of interaction among people in the group is itself the primary objective of practice. This process of interaction among people in the group may be stimulated at the beginning by a worker, and may be facilitated at certain stages of the group's development by a worker, but it is outside the worker's control. It is possible to describe such a process of interaction among people in a group at some stage as a process of community or as a process of emerging community.

Maxwell Jones (1979) described the origins of the idea and practice of 'therapeutic communities' at Maudsley Hospital in London in World War II. He was working with 'cardiac neurosis' in soldiers and concluded that working with a unit of one hundred soldiers, all with similar problems, seemed to demand that their problems be discussed with all one hundred men at the same time. Maxwell Jones recognised that the nursing staff who were working with the men came from different backgrounds and did not think as most nurses might be expected to think. They participated readily as members of a group. In general, wartime conditions helped to create a feeling of closeness and interdependence, of intimacy and democratisation. But for Maxwell Jones the most important lesson was that therapeutic communities had shown the importance of the patients' own peer group.[15]

Any presumption that the idea of community in therapeutic communities might run counter to the idea of individualisation of services was rejected by Colin Archer (1979), who insisted that the individualisation which is valued in social research was also reflected in therapeutic communities.[16] Another example of individualised services within the context of a supportive group process and self-help group activities was reported by Nicola Barry (1988) in *Social Work Today.* The Lothian Disabled People's Coalition was set up by disabled people as a self-help project to campaign for the rights and the needs of disabled people. At the same time, the Coalition emphasised the need for individual counselling and sought to provide it (as indeed many self-help groups do).[17]

The Cheshire Sexual Abuse Support Line was an example of social work with individual people – or 'clients' – developing into a group process to which the term 'community' might be applied. Melda Wilson (1989) described how the Support Line developed in 1986 from the practice of three social workers from Cheshire Social Services department who were working with women who had been sexually abused when young. The idea of group arose simply. Two clients of one of the social workers expressed an interest in meeting another victim of abuse. The social workers began by approaching women known to them as childhood victims of sex abuse. Very gradually they drew together a group and helped the women to articulate their experiences to each other. The scheme developed into a self-help group with the women, among other activities, producing a video on abuse to publicise the issue and help prevent abuse recurring. The social workers' role within the group changed from providing counselling to providing practical help and advice if it was needed.[18]

A similar example of social work with individual people developing into a group process was reported by Ian Weddle

(1991) in *Social Work Today*. It described how some social work practice in the field of mental health in Dumfries and Galloway in Scotland developed in the late 1980's. A social worker who was based at the principal hospital began to question the traditional casework approach which focussed on the hospital setting, and to look to work with people outside of the hospital – 'in the community' if you like. Becoming more aware of her clients' strengths she was encouraged to assist the development of long-term self-help groups. In 1989 the self-help groups came together in the Dumfries and Galloway Mental Health Association. The association built a clause into its constitution stipulating that no more than three professional workers could serve on the management committee. Among its subsequent activities the association produced a video promoting what it described as community mental health and developed a day care centre and promoted the provision of supported accommodation.[19]

However, group processes in health care and social work practice are not all-inclusive. Not everyone will respond or adapt; not everyone will want to belong; not everyone will want to go in or stay in. Readiness or reluctance to go in or stay in will vary, not only between one person and another, but also within one person at different stages of his or her own life and according to the nature and size of the group situation. Stuart Whitely (1979) observed that people who were suffering from schizophrenia which has led to hallucinations and delusions could participate in therapeutic communities when people who were withdrawn and apathetic could not.[20] Lami Mulvey and Vicki Hobson (1992) described the early withdrawal of some people from a self-help group established as part of a network of resources "within the community" which were intended to be local, accessible and based on self-definition of needs. Those who attended the self-help group chose the topics for discussion themselves. However, by the fourth week three people had withdrawn. One of those who withdrew explained that she had felt unable to talk about her problems within the group because it had been too large. [21] .

Community as a process of self-help and mutual support

Some of the projects described above had their origins in social work practice with individual persons. In time they developed as groups which offered a variety of support to people who participated in them: not only through one-to-one counselling, but also through sharing concerns and supporting each other in group activity.

Of course, such a process of self-help and mutual support through group activity does not begin necessarily with or arise from the intervention of outside workers or helpers. Sometimes a worker may play a significant role in helping people to come together. More often a group of people with common concerns will come together on their own initiative to share concerns, give support to each other or organise activities and services for each other.

The Community Development Foundation in a 1988 report [22] described the Broxtowe Better Way to Health Group, a notable example of self-help growing from simple beginnings. The group began early in 1982 when three women from the Broxtowe estate in Nottingham asked a local worker for help in setting up a keep fit group. They were interested in getting out of the house, in letting off steam, in learning about health. And they were determined to run the group themselves.

Premises were found in a local hall, a grant for operating expenses was obtained from the Social Services Department, and local publicity was launched. As the group developed, they decided to place greater emphasis on health education. Training courses were organised and booklets produced. The group developed a constitutional, self-managing structure with elections, management committee and monthly feedback to members.

Ligoniel Family Centre in the Ligoniel area of North Belfast has been another example of the planning and eventual development of a major centre by the women who use it. The idea for the centre arose among a group of local women, mostly with young children, who had been attending a mothers and toddlers group once a week in a local hall in the early 1980's. They wanted more for themselves and for their children. They wanted especially a permanent base of their own which they would manage themselves.

In 1988 the Northern Ireland Housing Executive made available a vacant four-bedroom house in the area at a nominal rent. It opened in October 1986 as Ligoniel Family Centre, offering a drop-in centre for mothers and children, with play activities for children and classes in a variety of subjects, ranging from crocheting to health education for the women. The centre grew in terms of numbers attending and the demands being placed on the voluntary committee of local women which managed it. In September 1989 a co-ordinator and four playworkers (later increased to six) were appointed with the help of funding from the Belfast Action teams programme and various trusts.

The numbers attending and the range of activities continued to grow, so in 1991 a second vacant house was obtained by the committee from the Northern Ireland Housing Executive, as a base for the co-ordinator. The first house became a base for children's play activities.

Subsequently the activities and services of the centre developed beyond the original further education classes and play activities to include respite for parents under stress; a regular, inexpensive lunch service for women and children attending (12,000 meals served in 1994-1995); advice and counselling services; a health care programme based on tasks, discussion groups and individual advice-giving; an after schools group and a group for young adolescent girls in the area. These activities and services arose from the ideas of the women attending the centre.[23]

A 1993 evaluation report spoke of the open door spirit of the centre and its non-lecturing atmosphere. It allowed "space for the natural and gradual development of relationships." Anyone who attended the family centre and who was registered with it was accepted as a member with voting rights, not a 'client'.[24]

A strong assertion of the benefits and the principles of self-help and mutual support was offered by Gillian Pascall (1986) when discussing Women's Aid refuges. She said that they were something new: not only did they offer accommodation and accept women's own assessment of their need; they offered community instead of bureaucracy, hierarchy and authority.[25]

Liz McShane (1993) in her report on the Community Support Programme in Northern Ireland, highlighted a range of self-help groups which offered different models of participation. The impetus behind the formation of the Northern Ireland Deaf Youth Association came from a group of young deaf people who wanted to overcome their isolation and improve their quality of life in the community, and who felt that deaf people should tackle these issues themselves.[26] The Newry and Mourne Carers' Association sought to meet the needs of carers by providing information on the services which were available, and by organising a relief service for carers and mutual support groups, social events and a quarterly news sheet.[27] PANDA – the 'People's Alternative to Narcotics, Drugs and Alcohol' – aimed to support people recovering from drug and alcohol abuse by offering them somewhere safe and welcoming to go to which they could contribute. It organised a drop-in centre with a management committee, the majority of whose members were themselves users of the centre. One veteran user of the centre observed how people might come in to the centre for the first time who were "practically unable to socialise"; and yet within perhaps a year they were sitting on the management committee and speaking out and making decisions.[28]

What is the essence of self-help groups such as these? It is not that they operate separately from or in opposition to professional workers. Many operate in co-operation with them. It is not that their own particular areas of interest, or their use of group processes, are different. Other kinds of group or organisation may share the same interests and also may make use of group processes to achieve their purpose. The essence of such self-help groups, I would argue, is in two elements:

(1) Broadly speaking, people control their own entry into and career through them; and because of this essential characteristic people in them are enabled to fill different roles rather than be confined indefinitely to the role of passive consumer of helping services. People choose their own helping relationships.

(2) The very process by which the groups form and operate, by which people come together, share concerns, support each other and organise together, could be described as a process of 'community'. Inasmuch as the idea of community is relevant, it could be applied to the very process of association.

REFERENCES

1. BOOTH, Tim, BOOTH, Wendy, and SIMON, Ken. (1990). *Outward bound : relocation and community care for people with learning disabilities.* Milton Keynes: Open University Press. p.178
2. *ibid.* pp.179-183
3. WARD, Linda. (1992). Foreword, *Normalisation : a reader for the Nineties.* Edited by Hilary Brown and Helen Smith. London: Tavistock/Routledge. Foreword. p.x
4. DALLEY, Gillian. (1992). Social welfare, ideology and normalisation, *Normalisation : a reader for the Nineties.* p.104
5. EMERSON, Eric. (1992). What is normalisation, *Normalisation : a reader for the Nineties.* p.3
6. SZIVAS, Sue. (1992). The limits of integration, *Normalisation : a reader for the Nineties.* p.112
7. EMERSON, Eric, and HUTTON, Chris. (1994). *Moving out : relocation from hospital to community.* London: HMSO. p.35
8. POWELL, Angela. (1992). Handsworth Community Care Centre, *Experiences of community care : case studies of UK practice.* Edited by Bruce Lynch and Richard Perry. Harlow: Longman. pp.78-85
9. ALLAN, Shula, and MORRIS, B. (1993). Oasis : the Mental Health in Community project, *Experiences of community care : case studies in UK practice.* pp.55-57
10. SIMIC, Paul. (1994). Moving out of hospital into the community, *Caring for people in the community : the new welfare.* Edited by Michael Titterton. London: Jessica Kingsley. pp.67-68
11. MORRIS, Jenny. (1993). *Independent lives : community care and disabled people.* Basingstoke: Macmillan. pp.55-65

12. McKNIGHT, John L. (1992). Redefining community, *Social Policy* (New York: Social Policy Corporation). Vol.23, no.2 (Fall-Winter 1992). pp.56-57

13. TYNE, Alan. (1992). Normalisation : from theory to practice, *Normalisation : a reader for the Nineties.* p.36

14. GRIFFITHS, Jonathan. (1978). *Community Care : Supplement.*

    (Sutton: IPC Business)

15. JONES, Maxwell. (1979). The therapeutic community : social learning and change, *Therapeutic communities : reflections and progress.* Edited by R.D. Hinshelwood and N. Manning. London: Routledge & Kegan Paul. p.6

16. ARCHER, Colin. (1979). The therapeutic community in a local authority day care programme, *Therapeutic communities : reflections and progress.* p.33

17. BARRY, Nicola. (1988). Making the connection, *Social Work Today* (London: Macmillan Magazines) (21 July 1988). p.19

18. WILSON, Melda. (1989). Overcoming the legacy of child sex abuse, *Social Work Today* (6 April 1989). pp.12-13

19. WEDDLE, Ian. (1991). Making the connection, *Social Work Today* (4 July 1991). pp.15-17

20. WHITELY, Stuart. (1979). Progress and reflection, *Therapeutic communities : reflections and progress.* p.18

21. HOBSON, Vicki, and MULVEY, Lami. (1992). Craigentinney Health Project, *Experiences of community care : case studies in UK practice.* pp.63-77

22. COMMUNITY PROJECTS Foundation. (1988). *Action for health : initiatives in local communities.* London: Community Projects Foundation. pp.44-45

23. Ligoniel Family Centre (Belfast) annual reports (1995-1997)

24. O'KEEFE, Peigi. (1993). *Ligoniel Family Centre (Belfast) evaluation report*

25. PASCALL, Gillian. (1986). *Social policy : a feminist analysis.* London: Tavistock. Repr. Routledge, 1991 & 1994. p.162

26. McSHANE, Liz. (1993). *Community support : a pilot programme.* Belfast: Northern Ireland Voluntary Trust. p.129

27. *ibid.* pp.46-47

28. *ibid.* pp.42-43, 101

3

AREA REGENERATION PROGRAMMES

The focus of area regeneration programmes – Locality and community in area regeneration programmes – How are areas chosen?: locality as a basis for aid programmes – Assumptions about community : about membership and cohesiveness

The focus of area regeneration programmes

In 1968 the Seebohm Report on the Personal Social Services in England and Wales expressed concern about " ... recognised problem areas lacking a sense of community." [1] The area regeneration programmes discussed here were focussed on certain areas and were designed to direct additional resources or new ways of administering or delivering services to address problems or needs from which some people suffered: such as poverty and low income, or sub-standard housing and inadequate living conditions, or lack of training and employment opportunities, or the decline of some urban and rural areas.

John Edwards and Richard Batley (1978) saw these programmes as being a phenomenon originating in the 1960's and 1970's.[2] In the 1960's, the Education Priority Areas programme sought to tackle poverty through educational remedies.[3] The Urban Programme, launched in 1968, sought to tackle poverty and urban decline through a variety of projects. Under the umbrella of the European Community the 1970's saw the introduction of the first pilot schemes to combat poverty.[4] In Northern Ireland in the 1970's, unemployment and low income were central to the analysis of social need which prefigured the Belfast Areas of Need programme, which was succeeded in turn by the Belfast Action Teams and Making Belfast Work programmes.[5]

In the 1960's, concern with housing problems - with overcrowding, physical decay of housing stock, and lack of amenities for residents - prompted the establishment of General Improvement Areas, followed by Housing Action Areas in the

1970's, and the development of the strategy of decentralised estate management.[6]

Often the area regeneration programmes and the policies and analyses of social need which they reflected promoted a sense that certain areas suffered from a multiplicity of problems, not simply one or two. In the 1960's, the criteria for identifying education priority areas included occupation, income, family size and housing conditions as well as the incidence of physical disability and learning disabilities.[7] In 1968 the Seebohm Report spoke of the need to encourage the development of community identity in areas, which, it considered, were characterised by rapid population turnover, high delinquency, child deprivation and mental illness and other indices of 'social pathology'.[8] In 1974 a Home Office circular on the Urban Programme referred to areas of special need which it considered to be characterised by poverty, high levels of unemployment, overcrowding, old dilapidated housing, delinquency, mental disorder and children in care.[9] In 1977 the White Paper *Policy for the Inner Cities* linked economic decline, physical decay and social disadvantage as factors in the perceived decline of inner city areas. Nicholas Deakin and John Edwards, writing in 1993, observed that current strategy on the inner cities, which at that time included the Urban Programme, Urban Development Corporations, Task Forces, City Action Teams and Enterprise Zones assumed the existence of areas which were characterised by social, physical and economic decay, and were relatively insulated in their decay.[10] Suzanne McGregor in 1995 judged the City Challenge Programme to be a response to the problems of areas which had been stigmatised.[11]

Whatever is the particular problem or issue which is the subject of an area regeneration programme, such programmes often have core strategies of concentrating resources in particular geographical areas, and of emphasising the relevance of community to the programme. Community as discussed or referred to in area regeneration programmes is an umbrella term which covers a variety of concerns and objectives. It may be used to describe initiatives from a group of people who are the subject of the programme (*e.g.* 'community projects'). It may refer to the accountability of public bodies or agencies administering programmes to people who are the subject of the programme (*e.g.* 'accountability to the community').

Locality and local community in area regeneration programmes

The most common expression of the idea of community in area regeneration programmes is the association of locality with community in the idea of 'local community'. For example, in Northern Ireland the Inter-Departmental Committee on Rural Development in 1990 advocated that an emphasis in rural development programmes should be placed on "the initiatives of local communities".[12] The Making Belfast Work Strategy Statement of March 1995 considered that the success of the programme would depend on the positive support and involvement of the local community.[13] In 1988 the corporate plan of the Trafford Park Urban Development Corporation in Manchester declared one of its objectives to be the translation of the benefits of economic activity to "the local community".[14]

The Department of the Environment claimed that the City Challenge Programme, launched in June 1991, gave people the power to shape the future of their areas – for the first time.[15] In 1995 the Department of the Environment sought to define what it meant by community in the regeneration programmes – the Single Regeneration Budget Challenge Fund, City Challenge, Housing Action Trusts, Task Forces, Rural Challenge, Rural Development Programmes – which it sponsored. It acknowledged that the regeneration programmes were intended to benefit defined areas, and it stated that the people living or working within each target area constituted the community as far as the particular programme for that area was concerned.[16]

'Local community' has been a central idea in regeneration programmes: in the reports, commentaries and statements which have been issued concerning the programmes. But the link between locality and community tends to be assumed without being analysed or justified. The persistent emphasis on local community represents an assumption of common relationships, associations and institutions between the people who are resident in particular localities. Therefore, I believe that it is appropriate to look at the choice of locality, of defined areas, as a basis for regeneration programmes and then to ask: is the idea of community needed?

How are areas chosen? Locality as a basis for regeneration programmes

Usually areas which are chosen as subjects of regeneration programmes have a higher than average concentration of certain social problems according to the various indicators on need which are used. In the 1960's, as noted above, the criteria for identifying education priority areas included occupation, income, family size and housing conditions as well as physical disability and learning disabilities. The Home Office in 1974 considered that the areas of special need which were the concern of the Urban Programme to be characterised by poverty, high levels of unemployment, overcrowding, old and dilapidated housing, mental disorder and children in care. The 1992 evaluation report on the Belfast Action Teams noted that resources were allocated to the action team areas very much in relation to need as measured by indices of deprivation. Action teams were assigned first to the most deprived inner areas of Belfast.[17]

It is, I would suggest, a crucial feature of the processes of selection and of the criteria used, that areas of special need are identified by the concentration of individual problems, *i.e.* problems which are experienced individually by each person. Unemployment, underemployment, poor housing, access to transport, low income are all circumstances of individual people and families, even if they have consequences for social relations or have structural causes. The process of identification of areas as areas of need does not depend on, is not related to, any pattern of social relations or any common organisation or common identity which might be implied by the word community. Community is not the basis for defining need or identifying areas of need. (An interesting variation to this trend was presented by the City Challenge programme which focussed on particular neighbourhoods or communities. A 1992 Note from the Department of the Environment advised that the community in the programme comprised anyone who has a financial or personal investment in the area – residents, shopkeepers, parents, unemployed people, tenants, young people, students and visitors.[18]

The contradiction between, on the one hand an individualised basis for identifying areas of need, and on the other hand an advocacy of community involvement or community participation, is evident in Derek Birrell's and Carol Wilson's 1993 critique of the Making Belfast Work Programme. On the one hand they sought a more efficient statement of levels of individual need, and so a more precise definition of areas of need.[19] On the other hand they found that the record of the programme on community involvement was patchy and that no means had been established to allow communities to express needs or influence projects.[20] They did not consider how these two objectives related to each other or if they related to each other; and whether striving towards one objective might sustain or might undermine the other objective. For example: if communities – or people and groups as communities – went further in expressing needs and influencing projects, how could it be assumed that how they saw themselves and what projects they advocated would fit neatly within the framework offered by the more precisely defined areas of need as referred to above?

An interesting historical precedent in Ireland for the area regeneration programmes is the Congested Districts Board, which shed some light by comparison and by contrast with later aid programmes. The Congested Districts Board was created by Arthur Balfour, then Chief Secretary for Ireland, in 1891. It was finally abolished by the new Irish government in 1923. The Board's resources and activities were directed at "... certain areas of exceptional poverty" in the West of Ireland.[21] It was concerned with areas perceived as being overcrowded and threatened with famine. The criteria for identifying areas was simple; an average rateable value of less than thirty shillings per head. The programme was managed by a centrally appointed board. Much of the board's expenditure was on infrastructure projects such as the building or improvement of railways, harbours, roads or bridges. It supported current activities and promoted new activities.[22]

The particular relevance of the Congested Districts Board in relation to the present subject of discussion is in the comparison of an aid programme in selected geographical areas where there was perceived to be an especially high concentration of need and the contrast of an aid programme in which there was no element of the idea of community in defining need, and (as far as can be ascertained) no use of the word community.

The identification of specific areas as being problem areas has been called into question over the years. For example, Peter Townsend (1976) questioned the area strategy for tackling poverty. He argued that in most areas which had been identified as priority areas, more people were not deprived than were deprived.[23] Paul Knox (1989), while acknowledging that there were significant differences between particular areas, insisted that many people who might be considered disadvantaged or vulnerable or victimised did not live in identified problem areas.[24] Justin Beaumont and Chris Hamnett (2001), reported on research in the London borough of Lambeth as part of an international research project for the European Commission. The report found that differences between the apparently poor north and affluent south of Lambeth were relative. There were affluent people living in the north of the borough and poor people living in the south.[25] Michael Gibson and Michael Langstaff (1982), in referring to the debates on poverty in the 1960's, and the growth of the priority areas approach, argued that there was no evidence to suggest that a majority or even significant proportion of the millions of people in poverty lived in these small areas.[26]

The idea of community and related ideas of communication, self help, accountability, consultation and participation

'Community' in relation to regeneration programmes tends to stand for people outside of government, public bodies and private institutions. Community in relation to regeneration programmes is linked usually to other ideas of communication between people and government, and partnership between people and outside bodies; of self help by people experiencing problems; of accountability by government and non-government agencies to people affected by their decisions; and of consultation with people about the decisions which affect them and participation by them in the decision making process.

Often the idea of local community is linked to these other ideas. Indeed as the above quotations suggest, local community is likely to be seen as the principal framework for applying these other ideas of communication or partnership or self-help or accountability or consultation and participation.

'Community' may be used to indicate an all embracing social network or organisation, or a series of smaller scale social networks or organisations. A notable example was the Making Belfast Work Strategy Statement issued by the Northern Ireland Government in 1995.[27] Within its sixteen pages of text it referred to 'community', 'communities' or 'local communities' fifteen times. It expressed concern for the "communities in greatest decline" (p.6) and a determination to give 'communities' a real say in the policies which affect their daily lives (p.3). It sought to promote partnerships which had to be open and accountable to "local communities ... and the wider community" (p.12).

Assumptions about community : about membership and cohesiveness

But often what is meant by local community is not discussed. And most often who is included within the community or within particular communities, and on what basis they are included, is not discussed. This common failure to discuss what is meant by local community and who is included carries with it assumptions about membership and cohesiveness. It seems to be assumed that when talking of community in relation to a particular place – whether that place is a housing estate, or a neighbourhood or a town, or a rural townland or whatever – that the people who live within that area are part of the community. They are, in a sense, members of that community.

Along with the assumption of membership of the community, there tends to be an assumption of cohesiveness: or assumptions that people of that area have common interests, common outlooks, common associations, common responses to proposals from government or from other outside bodies. Such assumptions of cohesiveness are evident in the statements about and the statements from area regeneration programmes, as quoted above.

Assumptions of membership and cohesiveness can be called into question even when there appears to be a strong sense of community. Graham Day's and Jonathan Murdoch's study of the Ithon Valley in Mid Wales (1993) illustrated how institutions and forms of social life within a particular community may be dominated by a particular group with elements of tension or conflict or exclusion.[28] They found also that women's experience of community in the valley could be negative. If women sought employment, they found it necessary to travel to a nearby town, which made it difficult for young women to remain in the area – unless they married into a farming family.

This negative experience of community for women in the valley in relation to employment prospects and the terms of their continued residence in the valley had some echo in the experience of women in South Armagh in Northern Ireland, as highlighted by Carmel Bradley and Avila Kilmurray (1991).[29] Although women's continued residence in the area on independent terms did not appear as an issue as it did for the women in the Ithon Valley, and although the majority of the women who were interviewed expressed a strong sense of commitment to the area, they expressed also a need for activities and services directed specifically at women. There was not a simple, unitary community. And a number of women who were interviewed for the survey requested that their separated or unmarried mother status should not be noted in the report. Their sense of community was not so inclusive that they could admit readily to their particular personal circumstances.

Michael Langstaff and Michael Gibson (1982) doubted that people would necessarily react as a cohesive or unitary community to threatened changes in their environment. They referred to studies of redevelopment in Leeds and Liverpool to attack what they described as two myths about redevelopment. The first myth was that every older housing area contained a cohesive community implacably opposed to clearance and rehousing. The second myth was that every older housing area contained residents who would welcome universally clearance and rehousing into modern public housing. In reality, they insisted, attitudes were based – person by person or family by family – on weighing the net gains and losses of moving or staying.[30]

REFERENCES

1. *REPORT of the Committee on Local Authority and Allied Personal Services* [Seebohm Report]. (1968). London: HMSO. paras. 453 & 486

2. BATLEY, Richard, and EDWARDS, John. (1978). *The politics of positive discrimination.* London: Tavistock. p.9

3. HALSEY, A.H. (1972). *Educational priority : EPA problems and policies.* London: HMSO for the Department of Education and Science. p.14

4. HILL, Malcolm (ed.). (1991). *Social work and the European Community.* London: Jessica Kingsley. pp.25-6

5a. P.A CAMBRIDGE Economic Consultants. (1977). *Belfast Areas of Special Need : report of Project Team.* Belfast: HMSO

5b. *Analysis of the Belfast Action Teams initiative.* (1977). Belfast: HMSO

5c. *Making Belfast Work strategy statement.* (1995). Belfast: Making Belfast Work. pp.28-32

6. BATLEY, Richard, and EDWARDS, John. (1978). *The politics of positive discrimination.* pp.17-19

7. *ibid.* pp.xi, 2, 48

8. Seebohm Report. (1968). para.477

9. HOME Office. (1974). *Urban Programme*. London: Home Office. (Circular ; 11)

10. DEAKIN, Nicholas, and EDWARDS, John. (1993). *The enterprise culture and the inner city*. London: Routledge. p.9

11. McGREGOR, Suzanne. *(1995).* Poverty, mega cities and social development, *Social policy and the city*. Edited by Helen Jones and John Lansley. Aldershot: Avebury. p.55

12. GREER, J.V, and MURRAY, M.R. (1991). Integrated rural development in Northern Ireland, *Business Outlook and Economic Review* (Belfast: First Trust Bank). Vol.6, no.3 (November 1991)

13. *MAKING Belfast Work strategy statement*. (1995)

14. DEAKIN, Nicholas, and EDWARDS, John. (1993). *The Enterprise culture and the inner city*. London: Routledge. p.75

15. ENVIRONMENT, Department of the (Great Britain). (1991). Press release of 31st July 1991, quoted in: City challenge : the role of community involvement / John Mabbott, *Policy Studies* (London: Policy Studies Institute). Vol.14, no.2 (Summer 1993) p.27

16. ENVIRONMENT, Department of the (Great Britain). (1995). *Involving communities in urban and rural regeneration : a guide for practitioners*. Ruislip: Department of the Environment. para.2.2

17. P.A. CAMBRIDGE Economic Consultants. (1992). *Analysis of the Belfast Action Teams initiative*. Belfast: HMSO. para.11.1, p.71

18. McGREGOR, Suzanne. (1995). Poverty, mega cities and social development. p.57

19. BIRRELL, Derek, and WILSON, Carol. (1993). Making Belfast Work : an evaluation of an urban strategy, *Administration* (Dublin: Institute of Public Administration). Vol.41, no.1 (Spring 1993), p.54

20. *ibid.* p.51

21. BECKETT, J.C. (1966). *The making of modern Ireland*. London: Faber & Faber. p.408

22a. *ibid.* pp.408-9

22b. HUNTER, James. (1976). *The making of the crofting community.* Edinburgh: John Donald. pp.184-5

22c. FOSTER, R.F. (1989). *Modern Ireland, 1600-1972.* London: Penguin. pp.456, 614

23. TOWNSEND, Peter. (1976). Area deprivation policies, *New Statesman* (London). 6th August 1976. p.170

24. KNOX, Paul. (1989). The vulnerable, the victimised, the disadvantaged : who they are and where they live, *Social problems and the city.* Edited by David T. Herbert and David M. Smith. Oxford: Oxford University Press. p.40

25. BEAUMONT, Justin, and HAMNETT, Chris. (2001). *The spatial dimensions of urban social exclusion and integration : the case of London, United Kingdom.* Amsterdam: University of Amsterdam. (http://www.frw.uva.nl/ame/urbex). pp.15-18. (URBEX series ; 15)

26. GIBSON, Michael, and LANGSTAFF, Michael. (1982). *An Introduction to urban renewal.* p.140

27. *MAKING Belfast Work strategy statement.*

28. DAY, Graham, and MURDOCH, Jonathan. (1993). Locality and community ; coming to terms with place, *Sociological Review* (London: Routledge & Kegan Paul). Vol.41, no.1 (February 1993). p.99

29. BRADLEY, Carmel, and KILMURRAY, Avila (eds.). (1989). *Rural women in South Armagh : needs and aspirations.* Belfast: Rural Action Project, 1989, repr. 1991. p.16

30. GIBSON, Michael, and LANGSTAFF, Michael. (1982). *An introduction to urban renewal.* p.45

Part 2:

Is there such a thing as community?

4

IS HUMAN NATURE INDIVIDUAL OR SOC
COMMUNITY, ASSOCIATION OR THE S
ARTIFICIAL?

Two ways of looking at our social experience and
The facts of existence : are there only individu
individual lives? – The facts of existence : i
altruism and co-operation – The biological facts
life, genes and what we are. – Evolution and here
may have come to be what we are - What can biol
tell us about a person? – The puzzle of altr
operation : how do they come to be? – When did co-operation between human beings evolve? – Did co-operation evolve long before the arrival of human beings? - Or did co-operation evolve after the arrival of human beings? – Are we at the point where co-operation and altruism have evolved to become part of our nature? – Or is self-interest still the driving force of human affairs? – Altruistic actions as motivated actions : is altruism real? – If altruism and co-operation evolved : from what did they evolve? – Conclusion

> No man is an island, entire of itself; every man is a piece of the Continent, a part of the main ... any man's death diminishes me, because I am involved in mankind; and therefore never send to know for whom the bell tolls; it tolls for thee.
>
> John Donne, *Devotions upon Emergent Occasions*

> I have a cloak, close-wrapped and long;
> And a stout tower with door of steel,
> No way in for the bitter wind,
> Or piercing joy.
>
> Anneke Peters, *The Rock and the Island*

Two ways of looking at our social experience and our nature

"Community", declared Raymond Plant (1974), "is a very complex and contested meaning which we place upon our social experience." [1]

Few of us do not acknowledge the idea of community in some way or another. But more often than not we talk about community or refer to it or simply use the word without asking: is this a valid way of describing our social experience? Is it an appropriate idea to apply to the forms of association with other people in which we are involved, whether they are small groups or larger associations, or personal networks or 'society'?

There are two ways of looking at our social experience, at our interaction with and our relations with other people, that are completely different from each other. In the first view the forms of association with other people in which we are involved are no more than arrangements which are necessary in order to protect and advance our individual interests. Each person learns to co-operate with other people as the sometimes necessary means to the ends of self-protection and self-advancement. Acts of co-operation are more likely to occur when each person who is concerned benefits directly from the process. Help is given to other people on an expectation of help being received, when needed, in the future.

An alternative view is that the forms of association in which we are involved with other people are part of what and who we are. Co-operation with other people is a fact of our existence from our beginnings. It is natural for us to live in groups in association with other people because it is necessary for our development as human beings. We are highly social creatures. The forms of association in which we are involved help to express what and who we are, as well as helping to meet individual needs. So it may be realistic within such a perspective to talk about community.

These two different ways of looking at our social experience represent two different views of human nature, of what we are : we are individualist creatures or we are social creatures. And what we are refers not only to the physical facts of our existence, but also our mental states; and not only our individual mental states, but also our perceptions of and our interaction with each other; and not only our perceptions of and our interaction with each other at any one time, but also the ways of thinking and of doing things that we hand on to other people and to later generations.

We can examine these two perspectives – that we are individualist creatures or that we are social creatures – and ask: to what degree does either perspective correspond with reality: with what could be called the facts of existence?

The facts of existence: are there only individual people and individual lives?

Thomas Hobbes, the great seventeenth century philosopher of individuality, saw men as driven by individual desires, fears and ambitions. "... I put forward a general inclination of all mankind, a perpetual and restless desire of power after power, that ceaseth only on Death; and the cause of this is ... because he cannot assure the power and means to live well without the acquisition of more ..." [2]

Thomas Hobbes did not deny that men sought association with each other in society: "... to man by nature ... as soon as he is born, solitude is an enemy." [3] But men did not seek society for its own sake; rather they sought it for self-advancement and for security: "We do not therefore by nature seek society for its own sake, but that we may receive some honour or profit from it ..." [4] "The original of all great and lasting societies consisted not in the mutual goodwill men had towards each other, but in the mutual fear they had of each other ..." [5]

Although men needed society and sought society, they were not born prepared for it: "... all men, because they are born in infancy, are born inapt for society ... Wherefore man is made fit for society not by nature but by education ..." [6]

Thomas Hobbes conceived liberty and rights as essentially individual. The concession of liberty and rights to other people, within a contract, or to the ruler or state exercising political authority, was to extend only so far as was necessary for individual self-interest: "By liberty is understood the absence of external impediments: every man has a right to everything ... but he should be willing, when others are so ... to lay down the right to all things; and be contented with so much liberty against other men as he would allow other men against himself ..." [7] "No man giveth but with the intention of good to himself ..." [8]

For Thomas Hobbes a free man was a thoroughly individual entity: "A free man is he, that in those things, which by his own strength and wit he is able to do, is not hindered to do what he has a will to do ..." [9] (Women did not appear except marginally in the writings of Thomas Hobbes. But as Karen Green (1994) pointed out, the existence of women, and children, posed an immediate difficulty for his theories because of the significant imbalances of power in society.[10] You could not concede liberties and rights to others within a contract if you were not allowed to exercise those liberties and rights in the first place.)

In more recent times Robert Nozick (1974) argued for a minimal state which would be limited to the functions of protecting its citizens against force, theft and fraud and of enforcing contracts.[11] He insisted that there were only "different individual people with their own individual lives" so that it was not permissible that one person be sacrificed for others. On this basis he argued that it was as illegitimate for the state to take a man's goods through taxes to pay for services for needy people as it would be to direct him into forced labour to provide services for needy people.[12] He insisted also on what he described as the fact of our separate existences.[13] His conception of individual rights and the minimal state was based on the individualist perspective of human nature and existence.

The facts of existence: individualism, altruism and co-operation

Within the individualist perspective, forms of association between people are seen as collective means to individual ends. Human behaviour is motivated ultimately by self-interest. Help for other people and co-operation with other people arise in the beginning from calculations of self-interest.

If the individualist perspective is valid, if it corresponds to the facts of existence, then is there any sense in talking about community? It would be better perhaps to use simple terms (such as group or association) that indicate only people coming together for some common purpose, and do not make any claims about the quality of their relationships.

Robert Axelrod asked in *The Evolution of Co-operation* (1984): under what conditions would co-operation emerge in a world of egoists? After all (he argued) people tended to look after themselves and their own first.[14] But if they do, then altruistic and co-operative behaviours become problems: puzzles which need to be explained. (An action can be described as altruistic when it benefits an individual at the expense of the individual performing the action. Behaviour is co-operative when individuals act together for the benefit of each other.)

The factors which may lead to the emergence of altruistic and co-operative behaviour are the subject of continuing debate. They have been explained in terms of kinship, when individuals who help each other are related to each other;[15] and in terms of reciprocity, when help is given in the expectation of help being received when needed in the future.[16] But not all behaviour can be explained in terms of kinship and reciprocity. For example, more recently co-operative behaviour has been explained in terms of a recognition of and a response to shared characteristics,[17] and in terms of punishment of individuals who might defect from the group (because punishment can reinforce group solidarity).[18]

There is a common theme running through these perspectives. It is that altruistic and co-operative behaviours have emerged over time; they have *evolved*, in nature and among human beings. What we are is what we have evolved over time to be.

That altruism and co-operation between human beings, and between other organisms in nature, may have evolved over time introduces another theme: the role of biological processes in determining what we are. If what we are is what we have evolved to be, then what we are may be partly or largely the outcome of biological processes and the influence of our genes. For Edward Wilson (1978) biology was the key to understanding human nature. The question, he believed, was not whether or not human nature was genetically determined but rather: to what extent? [19] Jerome Barkow (1992) asserted that biological evolution underlies human psychology, and that human psychology underlies culture and society.[20]

If we discuss what we are purely in terms of social behaviour and our forms of association with each other, if we leave out biology, then there may always be the response: yes, we may appear to be social creatures, given the prevalence of group life and learning and of forms of association with each other. But what we appear to be now may be what we have evolved to be, and what we have evolved to be may represent biological imperatives in which individual self-interest was the original motive and remains the dominant motive.

It is important therefore to explore the biological facts of existence and especially what they may tell us about what we are: whether we are individualist creatures or social creatures. Firstly I will examine the biological facts of life and heredity; and then the significance of DNA and our genes.

The biological facts of existence: life, genes and what we are

Biological processes are part of the facts of existence. They are the processes by which life emerges and develops; by which different elements come together to form a living organism, whether it is a plant or insect or animal – or human being.

Living organisms come together, interact with each other and the environment, and reproduce. Reproduction is fundamental to life, or at least to the continued existence and development of life forms.

All life is composed of cells. Cells are the smallest units of which living tissue and organisms are composed. The major changes that occur in plants and animals and human beings come about as the result of changes in the properties of numerous cells.[21]

A cell is a complex and dynamic little structure. To understand something of what is happening all the time in each cell is to be impressed by the sheer intensity of the activity, as well as its complexity (*See* Glossary: Cells).

Much of the activity within the cell involves the synthesising of molecules. Molecules are groups of atoms which are bonded together to form a distinct unit (*See* Glossary: Atoms and Molecules). Molecules may consist of a few atoms or many. The giant molecules have been described by Steven Rose as "the stuff of life". [22]

Life is characterised by reproduction. It is characterised also by multiplication, division and complexity. Throughout our lives the cells of our bodies are dividing constantly.[23] Each cell in the adult body has its own life cycle from birth to death and replacement within a few days, weeks or months (Brain cells – neurons – may be exceptions to this rule. Most, but not all, last a lifetime).[24] During an average lifetime of seventy or eighty years, every cell in our body, apart from brain cells, will have died and been replaced many hundreds of thousands of times. The giant molecules will last for a few hours or days or months only to be broken down again and replaced by successor molecules which are exact or almost exact copies.[25]

In the nucleus of each succeeding cell are copies of the same DNA and the same genes. DNA (deoxyribonucleic acid) is the largest organic molecule. It has been described as a long set of instructions for building a body.[26] Genes are segments of DNA which have a function, although the function may vary from one situation to the next and from one time to another. Genes could be described as units of information. They give messages as to how things can be done. Most immediately, they give messages for (or 'encode for') the building of protein molecules, the basic building blocks of life and of organisms.

For some people, genes are of almost inspirational importance. Walter Gilbert (1992) referred to all of the genes which make up a human being. He considered that when the Human Genome Project, which seeks to map the entire sequences of human DNA, is completed, it could provide the answer to the question: what makes us human? [27] James Watson (1990) believed that our DNA molecules would provide "the ultimate answer to the chemical underpinnings of human existence." [28]

Evolution and heredity: how we may have come to be what we are

Many people consider genes to be at the centre of the theory of evolution; or that theory of evolution which is predominant today: the theory of Charles Darwin, which was first made public over one hundred and forty years ago. Charles Darwin asked: how did different kinds of organism (or 'organic being') develop in a state of nature, whether the organisms were plants or insects or animals – or human beings? How did species arise? How did organisms become adapted to each other and to the conditions of life? ("We see beautiful adaptations everywhere and in every part of the organic world") [29]

Charles Darwin concluded that different organisms, different species and adaptations to different conditions of life resulted from what he termed the universal struggle for life.[30] The struggle for life followed inevitably from the tendency of all organisms to increase in numbers to a size of population in excess of what their environment could sustain. Only a small number of each species could survive.[31] "Every single organic being around us may be said to be striving to the utmost to increase in numbers ... each lives by a struggle at some period of its life ... heavy destruction inevitably falls on the young and old during each generation, at recurrent intervals." [32]

In the struggle for life, any individual holding an advantage, however slight, would have a better chance of surviving and reproducing. Any variation in characteristics that gave an advantage to one organism over other organisms would be inherited by offspring of that organism. Therefore that organism and its offspring were more likely to grow in numbers over time than were other organisms. Any variation in characteristics that put an organism at a disadvantage compared to other organisms was likely to mean that that organism and its offspring would decline in numbers from one generation to the next compared to the other organisms and their offspring.

Variations could happen because of changes in the external conditions in which organisms existed, and the organisms' adaptation to those changes; or because of the simple fact that in each generation the child is not exactly similar to the parent.[33]

Charles Darwin applied the name 'natural selection' to the process by which variations, if they proved useful to an organism, could be preserved and increased as a proportion of the population. Natural selection, he asserted, was a power incessantly ready for action.[34] But the process did not happen quickly or simply. It happened by the accumulation of slight, successive, favourable variations over a very long period of time.[35]

Charles Darwin had difficulty in explaining the process of the inheritance of characteristics from one generation to the next.[36] He recognised that the offspring of organisms tended to inherit the characteristics of their parents; and therefore that the variations between the characteristics of their parents and the characteristics of other organisms of their parents' generation were passed to the next generation. But how did the process work? And how did it work in such a way that variations between organisms, and variations between groups of organisms, and the number and the range of groups of organisms, *increased* over the generations?

An answer emerged eventually as a result of experiments conducted by Gregor (born Johann) Mendel in the 1850's and 1860's. The theory of evolution as widely understood today represents a combination of Charles Darwin's theory of evolution and the findings of Gregor Mendel (the so-called 'modern synthesis').[37]

Johann Mendel was born in 1822 in the town of Brünn (later Brno) in Moravia. Later he entered the Augustinian monastery in the town and took the name of Gregor. He attended the University of Vienna for two years to 1853 and then returned to Brünn/Brno as a supply teacher in a local school. He conducted scientific experiments in his spare time. In 1868 he was elected abbot of the Augustinian monastery and became absorbed by the demands of administration. He died in 1884.[38]

Gregor Mendel conducted the experiments which made him famous (long after his death) on pea plants, because they suited his research purpose at the time. He divided pea plants into classes defined by different single, visible, easily distinguished characteristics: height, colour, type of flower and so on. He obtained pure breeding lines for each characteristic, and paired the pea plants according to opposite characteristics; for example: long/short; yellow seed/green seed; purple flower/white flower; and so on.

Gregor Mendel discovered that the inheritance of characteristics was not regular. If a plant with a particular characteristic was crossed with a plant with the opposite characteristic, then the offspring in the first generation would display only one characteristic. For example, if a tall plant was crossed with a short plant, then their first-generation offspring would be tall. If these hybrid tall plants were crossed with each other, then the short plant's characteristic re-emerged in their second-generation offspring, but not evenly. Their offspring of the second generation were tall and short in a ratio of approximately three to one.

Gregor Mendel concluded that there was a 'factor' controlling particular characteristics in each plant; and that when a plant displaying one particular characteristic was crossed with a plant displaying the opposite characteristic then the factor in one plant was dominant. However, the factor in the other plant did not disappear, but re-emerged in later generations. Nor did the two factors blend; they combined, but they remained distinct from each other. (This last point is especially important. If the 'factors' blended, then variations in characteristics would be lost gradually over the generations. Instead, these factors combine, but remain distinct from each other; and variations in characteristics are *conserved* over the generations).[39]

Today we know these 'factors' as genes, and we refer to dominant genes and recessive genes. Experiments since 1900 have demonstrated that the laws which Gregor Mendel discovered can be applied to a wide variety of characteristics in many different kinds of organisms.[40] His experimental findings have become the basis of the science of genetics. (Gregor Mendel's experiments and conclusions were neglected during his own lifetime. Peter Bowler (1989) has suggested that this was at least partly because he did not set out to discover new laws of heredity. He was interested in plant hybridisation rather than heredity; and he did not regard his experiments with pea plants as of being of the first importance.) [41]

Mark Ridley (1985) has asserted that all evolutionary changes start out as changes in genes.[42] Genes are passed from one generation to the next in the form of copies. What is copied is the 'sequence' of the gene, *i.e.* the order in which the different chemical components are arranged.

The copying of the sequence of genes from one generation to the next is an enormously complex process, and the copies are not perfect. Whether they are called mistakes or mutations or whatever, variations arise in the process of copying. The process of natural selection (so the theory goes) works on these variations. A useful, or successful, variation in the sequence of a gene is one which helps to give its organism (plant, insect, animal or human being) an advantage in the struggle for existence. An increased number of these 'successful' organisms means an increased number of the genes which contributed to that success. The adaptations to the organism spread, the organisms spread, the genes spread.

What can biology and genes tell us about a person?

For many people, genes are the key to how evolution works. Steven Pinker (1997) declared that the "gene's eye view" predominated in evolutionary biology. It had been asked, and was finding answers to, the deepest questions about life.[43] For Edward Wilson (1978), biology was the key to understanding human nature. The question, he believed, was not whether or not human social behaviour was determined genetically, but rather: to what extent? [44]

Some people believe that the study of twins, especially of identical twins, highlights the biological influence on human behaviour and human psychology. Steven Pinker (1997) believed that studies of identical twins demonstrated startling similarities between each twin in a pair, even among those twins who had been reared apart from each other. Those similarities, he suggested, cast doubt on the idea of the autonomous 'I'.[45]

Thomas J. Bouchard (1997), the founder of the University of Minnesota Centre for Twin and Adoption Research, described identical twins as true human clones: both born with exactly the same genes after the fertilised egg split in half. He reported that most identical twins who were reared apart from each other were similar to each other "in an astonishing range of psychological traits." [46]

However, twin studies demonstrated also the limits of the power of genes to shape psychological traits. Identical twins were less similar to each other than might be supposed. For example, with one pair of identical twins who were interviewed by the Centre, one was gay and the other was not. With another pair, one had contracted polio as a child and continued to walk with a limp; but the other had not. In general, identical twins continued to respond differently to many items on the questionnaire used by the Centre. For Thomas Bouchard, twin studies demonstrated the power of genes to shape psychological traits, but also the limits of that power.[47]

What can genes tell us about a person? Ralph Greenspan (1995) pointed out that researchers had failed to link specific human behaviour to solitary genes or small sets of genes.[48] He argued that well-controlled investigations on simple organisms suggested that a multiplicity of genes, some acting quite subtly, probably contributed to most behaviours. Ralph Greenspan based his argument on laboratory studies, including his own, of courtship patterns among fruit flies. He observed that most genes underlying courtship behaviour served a multiplicity of purposes. He concluded that there was every reason to believe that the genetic influence on behaviour would be at least as complicated in people as it was in fruit flies; and that the genetic influence on behaviour worked through many, multi-purpose and interacting genes, each making a small contribution.

The reality of our genetic heritage is of complexity, flexibility of response and unpredictability of outcome. Thomas Bouchard acknowledged that few behaviour geneticists believed that genes determined behaviour directly.[49] Philip Kitcher considered it a commonplace of genetics that the majority of traits of any organism – including human beings – resulted from the action of many genes and the interaction between the developing organism and its environment.[50] He noted that people wanted to know what had made it possible for us to "communicate with each other, compose string quartets, write poems, build cathedrals, harness sub-atomic sources of energy and study the interaction of molecules in living things." But, he insisted, nothing in our genetic sequence "was remotely likely to provide an answer."[51]

There are limits to the influence of our genes in determining human life. There are also significant limits to the influence of our genes in determining the malfunctioning of human life which is expressed in malignant diseases. The *New England Journal of Medicine* (2000) reported on a study of 44,788 pairs of twins born in Sweden, Denmark and Finland between 1886 and 1958. The study suggested that inherited genetic factors made a very minor contribution to the susceptibility of people to most types of cancer. The authors concluded that the overwhelmingly important factor in the occurrence of cancers in the population of twins studied was the environment. Only in cases of prostrate cancer, colorectal cancer and breast cancer did the evidence of the study suggest that inherited genetic factors made a significant contribution to susceptibility to the disease. Even then it was only in a minor proportion of cases that the risk of cancer could be explained by inherited genetic factors: forty-two percent for prostrate cancer, thirty-five percent for colorectal cancer and twenty-seven percent for breast cancer.[52]

The puzzle of altruism and co-operation: how do they come to be?

In the seventeenth century Thomas Hobbes insisted that "no man giveth but with the intention of good to himself." [53] Matt Ridley in *The Origins of Virtue* (1996) asserted that Thomas Hobbes' diagnosis was at the heart of modern evolutionary biology.[54] He quoted Karl Marx, John Maynard Keynes and Stephen Jay Gould in comparing competition between individual people in society, which provided the basis for economic activity and the evolution of economic structures, with competition between individual organisms in nature.[55]

And behind competition between individual people in society, behind competition between individual organisms in nature, was competition between individual genes. Genes were distinct from each other (and remained distinct from each other in the process of reproduction). Some were more successful than others in that they contributed more to the success of the organisms in the Darwinian struggle for existence. So genes were in a sense in competition with each other, and remained in competition with each other.

But if genes are distinct from each other; if they are in competition with each other; if they can be considered to be selfish or self-interested in how they move; and if they contribute decisively to their organisms' success in the struggle for existence: then how is altruistic or co-operative behaviour to be explained?

Altruistic behaviour is widespread in nature. Examples of altruistic actions are risking or accepting death to protect others; warning others of danger at a risk to oneself; sharing food; helping other adults with the rearing of their offspring. Altruistic behaviour is widespread in nature, but it appears to contradict Charles Darwin's theory of natural selection. The offspring of organisms which perform altruistic actions, it is supposed, ought to reduce in numbers over time compared to the offspring of other organisms. They should lose out in the struggle for existence.

How can altruistic actions evolve successfully into a pattern of behaviour? Edward Wilson (1975) described this question as the central theoretical problem of sociobiology. He explained altruistic behaviour in terms of genetic relatedness. It evolved most readily when those who performed altruistic actions and those who benefited from them were related; when they were kin. He referred to genes which caused altruism and genes which encoded for the tendency towards altruistic behaviour.[56]

But how could altruistic behaviour have evolved when helper and recipient were unrelated? Robert Trivers (1971) offered an explanation in the idea of reciprocal altruism. An individual organism performed altruistic actions in return for help given already, or in expectation of help to be given in return in the future. An individual organism may exchange altruistic actions and the benefits that come from them, so that over generations altruism is selected for, is favoured in the struggle for existence.[57]

As altruistic behaviour appears to contradict Charles Darwin's theory of natural selection, so does co-operative behaviour. Robert Axelrod and William Hamilton (1984) observed that co-operation was common in nature, between members of the same species and between members of different species.[58] They sought to explain co-operative behaviour in terms of kinship and reciprocity. Other explanations for co-operative actions when helper and recipient are unrelated have been advanced. For example, Rick Riolo, Michael Cohen and Robert Axelrod (2001) have drawn on computer simulations of encounters between people to argue that individuals co-operate with each other in response to shared characteristics: familiarity breeds co-operation.[59] Ernst Fehr and Simon Gächter (2002), drawing on experiments in group activity, argued that co-operation between people in groups could flourish if punishment of people who tried to defect from the group was allowed.[60]

Matt Ridley (1996) argued that the first life on earth was atomistic and individual; but increasingly organisms came together so that life became "a team game rather than a contest of loners." [61] If co-operation and co-operative behaviour can evolve from the material of individual self-interest, how does it happen? To explain this, some people have turned to games. Games theory refers to the organisation and study of games for what they may indicate about human behaviour and its outcomes in various carefully defined situations. Robert Axelrod (1984) used games to develop a theory of co-operation that could be used to discover what is necessary for co-operation to evolve.[62]

Perhaps the most famous, the most played and the most debated game is 'The Prisoner's Dilemma'. Two prisoners who have been accomplices face a choice: if one defects and confesses, he may gain an advantage over the other. But if both prisoners defect and confess, the benefit will be reduced. And if both co-operate, both can gain. For Peter Coveney and Roger Highfield (1995) the 'Prisoner's Dilemma' highlighted the conflict between the selfish desire of each player (or person) to pursue a 'winner takes all' philosophy, and the necessity of co-operation and compromise to advance that same interest.[63] It could be summarised as being concerned with situations in which you are tempted to do something for your own advantage, but in which it would be to each person's disadvantage if each person tried to do the same thing for his/her own individual advantage.

Given the starting conditions of the game, 'Prisoner's Dilemma' may encourage the conclusion that co-operation is illogical, in the sense that it is not in the individual person's self-interest. He/she may gain more if he/she acts on his/her own, and may lose if he/she seeks to co-operate only to find that the other person acts on his/her own. But strategies for playing and replaying the game suggest that co-operation would grow over time. Repeated interaction can bring recognition, association, reciprocity and a co-operative balance in the relations between people.

When did co-operation between human beings evolve?

So calculations of individual self-interest may lead to co-operative behaviour and co-operative forms of association; but if so, *when* did co-operation emerge in the history of the human species?

Perhaps a capacity for co-operation evolved *before* human beings emerged as a distinct species. Leda Cosmides and John Tooby (1992) believed that the human mind was the product of the evolutionary process, and they suggested that the capacity to think co-operatively and to enter into co-operative relations and co-operative forms of association with others had emerged as far back as 'our animal ancestors.' [64]

Perhaps other features of human social existence emerged as far back as our animal ancestors. Culture and the transmission of cultural traditions is an aspect of human social existence which had been thought to be unique by comparison with other species. Culture could be described as the passing on of ways of thinking about things and ways of doing things from one person to another and from one generation to the next by learning, by observation or by instruction; and then by doing. Culture and the transmission of cultural traditions depend on a capacity for co-operative behaviour and co-operative forms of association.

But culture is *not* a uniquely human phenomenon. Chimpanzees, our nearest relations within the animal kingdom, have rich and varied cultural traditions. Andrew Whiten and Christopher Boesch reported in *Scientific American* (January 2001) on their inquiry into chimpanzee cultures. They had sought the collaboration of every major research group studying chimpanzees. From different locations across Africa, they reported a multitude of distinct cultural patterns which were expressed in the use of tools, in forms of communication and in social customs.[65]

The cultural traditions among chimpanzees are much more elaborate than among any other animal species studied to date. But human customs and traditions are vastly more elaborate than those of chimpanzees. Perhaps language is a key to the difference. Andrew Whiten and Christopher Boesch pointed out that human customs and traditions are mediated by language.[66] Adam Kuper (1994) argued that the basic condition of human existence is that people are in communication with each other to a degree which is unique among primates. Furthermore, human beings have a capacity for symbolic communication. It allows them to talk about other times and other places, and to develop a sense that even people who are separated for long periods belong together. Consequently, human beings have a unique capacity to sustain relationships *in absentia*, while being apart from each other. They are released from a social existence bound by immediate returns and the necessity for continual reinforcement.[67]

Did co-operation evolve long before the arrival of human beings?

Perhaps co-operative behaviour and co-operative habits of thought evolved before the emergence of human beings as a distinct species. And perhaps co-operation and co-operative habits are even more ancient and fundamental to existence. Martin Nowak, Robert May and Karl Sigmund (1995) came to argue that co-operation was fundamental to existence from the earliest and most elementary life forms. Biologists, they pointed out, found examples of co-operation at the level of cells and even pre-biotic ('before life') molecules. And throughout the evolution of life, co-operation among smaller units has led to the emergence of more complex structures: for example, the emergence of multi-cellular creatures from single-cell organisms. Martin Nowak, Robert May and Karl Sigmund analysed evolutionary processes by performing computer simulations of processes in natural selection, testing strategies for survival and advancement. They found a definite trend towards co-operation throughout the evolution of life forms, from human beings to molecules. They imagined co-operation as being "older than life itself". [68]

Bacteria are among the oldest and most abundant organisms on earth, and are structurally very simple. But they do not exist as rugged individuals looking out for themselves and having little to say to each other. Bacteria can recognise and co-operate with their own kind. They demonstrate complex patterns of co-operative behaviour, and also of chemical communication or chemical signalling between each other and between themselves and more complex organisms.

The primitive history of co-operation has been described by Dale Kaiser and Richard Losick (1997) in their analysis of co-operation and communication between bacteria.[69] They reported that biologists had long understood that bacteria live in colonies. (In their article they alternated between referring to bacteria in colonies and bacteria in communities). Communication, co-operative behaviour and co-operative forms of association could develop in reaction to common concerns – often when nutrients began to run out. An outstanding example was MYXOCOCCUS XANTHUS, a species of bacteria that inhabits cultivated soil. When nutrients begin to run out, MX cells give out a chemical signal – 'factor A' – which indicates that the cell is short of nutrients. If only a few bacterial cells signal in this way, then it is understood that there is not a general problem; but when the signalling reaches a certain level of intensity, then it is understood that there is a general problem which requires common action. MX cells move "from different parts of the community" to gather at focal points. Then the cells begin to give out another chemical signal – 'factor C'. A certain high degree of factor C signalling indicates that optimum packing together of the cells has been achieved, and the cells stop moving together. Instead they activate the formation of spores which facilitate the movement of the 'community' to another location where more nutrients will be available.

Other bacteria may conduct "elaborate chemical conversations with higher organisms." An example is the soil dwelling RHIZOBIUM type of bacteria which through an elaborate process of signalling and counter signalling converts nitrogen gas from the atmosphere into a form which can be used by the leguminous plants which produce peas, soy beans and the like.

(Gregory Velicer, Lee Kroos and Richard Lenski have taken a rather different view of the MX bacteria. Their experiments led them to predict that cheating – obtaining benefits from the group in excess of what if anything they contributed – would be common in natural populations of MX. So MX bacteria exhibited both co-operative behaviour and individualist and cheating behaviour.)[70]

Or did co-operation evolve *after* the arrival of human beings?

Perhaps a capacity for co-operative behaviour evolved before the emergence of human beings as a distinct species. Or perhaps human beings developed a capacity for co-operation and co-operative habits of thought over time *after* they emerged as a distinct species.

Robert Trivers seemed to imply this in *Social Evolution* (1985) when he argued that the human capacity for sharing food, tools and knowledge, for helping the sick, the wounded and the very young developed in response to natural selection pressures. The characteristics of sharing, exchange, altruism and co-operation evolved over a very long time in response to conditions of existence in which people were living. This evolutionary process was especially likely to have developed during the long millennia of the Pleistocene Period (2,500,000 years ago to 10,000 years ago) when the conditions of human existence included a long life span, constant interaction in naturally dependent social groups, and extensive contacts with close relatives over many years.[71]

Matt Ridley seemed to imply this (that human beings developed a capacity for co-operation *after* they emerged as a distinct species) in *The Origins of Virtue* (1996), when he wrote of a time when human beings might have lived a life of self-sufficiency, able to survive without trading their skills for those of their fellow human beings.[72]

Matt Ridley drew a parallel between the increasing specialisation and interdependence of cells in bodies, which allowed for growth, and the increasing division of labour and interdependence between people and groups in society, which also allowed for growth.[73] The more connection there was between cells then the greater was the division of labour and specialisation of type between them. Bigger bodies tended to have more types of cell that were different from each other. The whole system was such that the self-interested ambition of each cell could only be satisfied by the cell doing its duty for the body. Equally, societies which became organised into larger groups tended to have more kinds of occupation. Specialisation and interdependence bred co-operation and co-operative habits of thought and action.

Are we at the point where co-operation and altruism have evolved to become part of our nature?

So perhaps co-operation is an outcome of the operation of self-interest. Organisms may discover over time that most often co-operation serves their self-interests and they become adapted to it in habits of thought as well as in actions. The process of natural selection may favour co-operation because these characteristics of organisms that are sympathetic to co-operation prove to be more successful over evolutionary time. Therefore we may have arrived at a point in our evolutionary development where co-operation has become part of our nature, of what we are.

But have human beings evolved from an earlier state of competition and conflict (organism v. organism / person v. person) to a point where we understand the benefits of co-operation and adapt to it in our social existence? Adam Kuper (1994) questioned the belief (which he associated with Thomas Hobbes) that the state of nature was a state of war; that the lives of people in ancient human communities, before the emergence of civil society and the state, was dominated by concern about war and peace, violence and security; that civil society developed in order to secure order and guarantee people the means of livelihood. He insisted that murderous violence against one's own kind, one's own species, was not unique to human beings: it could be observed, for example, among (those lovable) chimpanzees. And if contemporary hunter-gatherer bands could be seen as a kind of window for looking in on ancient human communities, which were based also on hunter-gatherer bands: then any perspective on ancient human communities had to take account of the fact that organised violence was in fact rare among contemporary hunter-gatherer bands.[74]

Adam Kuper (1994) did not accept that order was maintained in ancient or primitive communities, before the emergence of civil society and the state, simply because all the members of each group were related to each other. He did not accept that kinship was the cement of ancient communities. He pointed out that although members of contemporary hunter-gatherer bands are, as a rule, related to each other, common ancestry is not a pre-condition of membership. There are various routes to becoming a group member. Often a person will be a member of several groups during a lifetime. Some individuals live a peripatetic existence, between different groups.[75]

Or is self-interest still the driving force of human affairs?

But no matter when co-operation emerged, no matter how human beings, or other species before them, absorbed the lesson of co-operation – perhaps self-interest has remained a driving force in human affairs. Matt Ridley (1996) asserted that the first life on earth was atomistic and individual. Co-operation was used first of all to achieve selfish results.[76] Although there was (he believed) a gradual progression from individualism to co-operation in the evolution of life and social relationships, Matt Ridley could argue still that we had been designed to exploit the group for ourselves, rather than to sacrifice ourselves for the group.[77]

Explanations for apparently altruistic actions by people may be sought in terms of strategies of self-interest, as when explanations for altruistic actions by animals/other species are sought in terms of survival strategies. For example, Martin Bulmer in *Neighbours and Neighbouring* (1986), in which he examined the studies and the ideas of Philip Abrams and his team, noted that Philip Abrams had reacted against what he perceived to be the consensus that caring was primarily an altruistic activity. Philip Abrams believed that the idea of people wanting to help each other rested on a simple expectation of reciprocity.[78]

Edward Wilson (1990) saw a genetic basis for altruism and altruistic actions by human beings when he described the 'supposedly human' virtues of altruism and morality as being the survival strategies of our selfish genes.[79] Matt Ridley (1996), in arguing that selfish genes sometimes use selfless individuals to achieve their ends, proclaimed that "suddenly" altruism could be understood.[80]

There are major question marks against the idea that there may be a genetic basis for the apparent virtues of altruism or morality in human beings, or for apparently altruistic actions by human beings. Firstly there are the limits to the influence of our genes as discussed above. Secondly there is the place of values and the real element of choice in human actions which have an altruistic or moral character.

It may be argued that much human decision-making and actions of a moral or altruistic character reflects a pattern: the same decisions and the same actions by the same kind of people. Much decision-making of a moral or altruistic character may be considered to be habitual, reflecting conditioned responses. But although this argument may be considered valid in some or many situations, by itself it does not take account of conflicts of values. People can and do face, and are conscious of facing, real conflicts of values within themselves and between themselves and others about what to do in certain situations (see Chapter 8 below).

Furthermore, I would propose that choice is fundamental to life. For most if not all situations involving living organisms, there are alternative outcomes. Organisms have choice in the sense that in most situations they are faced with different possible courses of action and have a capacity to follow any one of them and to have some sense of the implications of their decisions.

People do make real choices: one person may face the same situation and the same choices as another person but choose to act differently from the other. Why will one person perform an altruistic action in a certain situation, but another person of similar background act differently in the same situation?

I would propose that different choices by different people about what to do in certain situations, and conflicts of values, are inherent in the very idea of values. Karl Popper (1976) believed that values emerged with problems: values could not exist without problems, and problems entered the world with life.[81]

Choice, values and conflicts of values do not contradict the idea of evolution. Mary Midgley (1994) saw human moral capacities as an evolutionary development – "... human moral capacities are just what could be expected to evolve when a highly social creature becomes intelligent enough to become aware of profound conflicts among its motives."[82]

Altruistic actions as motivated actions: is altruism real?

If what is described as an altruistic action between human beings is perceived as a motivated action, as a person knowingly doing something for others that did not benefit him or her, that may cost him or her, then the question can be asked: is the altruism real, or is it a reflection of longer term calculations of self-interest? It does not matter how long term an individual person's interpretation of his or her interests is, or what actions he or she undertakes which may benefit other people. If each person's motivation in engaging with other people is ultimately and always derived from some conception of his or her own interest, then altruism cannot be a valid way of describing each or any person's motivated action. And any forms of association between people will indicate only a need to seek support and advantage for individual ends through associations with other people.

Equally if altruism is real, if it can be considered as a valid description of the motivation for at least some actions by some people, then a simple individualist view of human nature, of what we are, cannot be sustained. And forms of association between people can express to some degree people's own natures and selves. This is not an issue of numbers (Do most people act altruistically or is altruism normal?); rather it is an issue of capacity: do some people act altruistically sometimes? Do they have the capacity for altruistic actions?

Barry Schwartz (1993) criticised comprehensively the rejection of altruism as a motive for human actions, asserting that altruism as a motive was real and pervasive.[83] He referred to general examples of altruism: where people put themselves in great physical danger to assist others; where people helped to hide Jews and others during the Holocaust (see also Chapter 11 for Norman Geras' study of Jewish rescue during the Holocaust); where bystanders intervened in situations in which they did not have a direct personal interest. This last example contrasted sharply with well-publicised examples of bystander apathy; but Barry Schwartz emphasised that the evidence leaned towards bystander intervention: usually people did help (pp.316-7).

Barry Schwartz drew on the use of games theory as a tool of research in social psychology, to examine people's actions and reactions in groups. He observed that people (in the controlled setting of games activity), shared responsibilities and co-operated on projects when neither was required by their immediate situations. The critical factor in determining whether co-operation occurred was whether people had opportunities to communicate with each other before they made their choices in the games activity; whether or not they had an opportunity to form a social bond. He concluded that: "it appears that if solidarity can form it will." (p.318)

So an important variable in determining the prevalence of altruistic behaviour was the degree of prior familiarity between people, or the lack of it. Another important variable was the cultural context of behaviour, as people reacted to the prevailing values in the society in which they lived (p.327). If for example, people perceived the prevailing values of their society to be individualist, they would be more inclined to identify with individualist motives for actions, and more inclined to choose actions according to individualist motives.

If altruism and co-operation evolved: from what did they evolve?

To argue that altruistic behaviour and co-operative behaviour have *evolved* is to argue in effect that human beings or other species, in their beginnings, acted and reacted on an individual basis from individual self-interest. If a particular behaviour evolved over time, then it evolved from a state of existence where people acted differently.

Mary Midgley (1994) questioned the idea that we begin simply as separate beings in competition with each other, and that the growing awareness of each other, and the bonds that are formed from that awareness, derive simply from calculations of self-interest. The awareness and the bonds went further, and signified more. Mary Midgley noted that the process of bonds being formed between people who originally were strangers to each other was common to all cultures.[84] But more than that, there is a positive capacity for sympathy, for entering directly into some of the feelings of the other person, and responding directly to them. Human beings have an ability to put themselves, imaginatively, in the place of other persons and to see "how it is" with them.[85]

Perhaps this idea of empathy is a matter of sentiment. But perhaps it has a biological basis. Vittorio Gallese and Alvin Goldman (1998) reported the discovery of a new class of neurons (brain cells): mirror neurons, which were observed first in monkeys. Mirror neurons are active when their owner performs particular actions. In itself this is unremarkable; but what is remarkable is that these mirror neurons are active also, they *respond* when their owner observes the same action being performed by another monkey. Experimental evidence has suggested that a similar process takes place with human beings.[86]

V.S. Ramachandran (2000) has speculated that mirror neurons could help to explain many puzzling questions about the evolution of the human brain and mind, *e.g.* mind reading and imitation learning, and even the evolution of language. He has argued that once you have the ability to read someone's intentions and the ability to mime their vocalisations, then you have set in motion the evolution of language.[87]

Conclusion

It can be argued that the many examples of co-operation and altruism suggest that co-operation and altruism are part of what we are: that they are natural.

On the other hand, it can be argued that all that examples of co-operation and altruism demonstrate is that various life forms, from the most elementary to the most complex – to human beings – discover in time that co-operation and helping others can be in their individual interest. In time they seek their individual self-interest by working for mutual advantage.

Within such a perspective, forms of association between people are collective means to individual ends. Matt Ridley (1996) argued that despite a gradual progression from individualism to co-operation and altruism in the evolution of life, we had been designed to exploit the group for ourselves rather than sacrifice ourselves for the group.[88] Robert Nozick (1974) asserted what he described as "the fact of our separate existences."[89]

Such a perspective represents a particular way of imagining the world: individual organisms are driven by self-interest and preoccupied with their own survival and advancement. Evolution involves a movement from a state of separate existence to a state of co-operative behaviour and co-operative habits of thought and co-operative forms of association.

John Maynard Smith (2000) suggested that several such movements may have taken place in evolutionary history. He proposed that the emergence of co-operation among our human ancestors was but the most recent among similar evolutionary movements (or 'flourishes') in which 'competitive entities' joined forces to form stronger, larger units upon which the process of natural selection could work.[90]

Such a view depends on a presumption: the presumption of original solitude. But is there or can there be or has there ever been a state of isolation, of original solitude, from which individual life forms emerge to enter into forms of association with each other? And is there or can there be, or has there ever been, a state of isolation, of original solitude in which individual human beings exist, from which they emerge to enter into forms of association with each other?

There is, I would argue, no evidence for any stage of human evolution which corresponds with such a picture of human existence. Various life forms, including human beings, may at certain times be especially aware of individual existence and act in pursuit of individual interests. At other times they may be aware of others, especially their own kind, and act co-operatively. Above all, it would seem that they are aware continuously of what they have in common and they act in response to that, depending on the circumstances. Evidence of behaviour which can be seen as an individual response to individual circumstances rather than group circumstances, is no proof of separate existence.

The idea that co-operation among human beings is something which has evolved introduces the question: when did it evolve? Perhaps it evolved before the emergence of human beings as a distinct species. Perhaps it evolved further back among primitive life forms. Or perhaps it evolved after the emergence of human beings as a distinct species.

The difficulties in answering this question – when did co-operation among human beings evolve? – may be because of the question itself. It seems to imply that co-operation and competition are different states of existence and that we move from one state of existence to another state of existence. Is this a realistic implication? Dale Kaiser and Richard Losick (1997) have described co-operation and communication between bacteria, which are among the oldest and simplest life forms on the planet (see above). They have described how cells of the MX bacteria come together and act together in response to common problems, *e.g.* a lack of nutrients. But Gregory Velicer, Lee Kroos and Richard Lenski (2001) have predicted that cheating would be common among natural populations of the MX bacteria (see above).

Who is right? Surely both are. They are not offering alternative explanations of the same behaviour, but rather explanations of different behaviours at different times. It is not: competition or co-operation; or: from competition to co-operation; but rather: co-operation and competition. Co-operative behaviour and competitive behaviour are recurrent and parallel themes of existence, from the earliest and most primitive life forms to human beings and human societies.

Co-operation and competition are fundamental to life. So, I would suggest, is choice. For every situation involving living organisms, there are alternative outcomes. Organisms have choice in the sense that in most situations, they are faced with different possible courses of action and have a capacity to follow any one of them, and to have some sense of the implications of what they decide. And if choice, as well as competition and co-operation, is fundamental to life, then our involvement in co-operative ideas, co-operative actions or co-operative forms of association cannot be explained simply as standard outcomes of a process of evolution: as conditioned responses.

Human beings as a species have not evolved from a state of individual existence to a state of social existence. Particular co-operative behaviours, or particular co-operative ways of thinking or particular co-operative structures may have evolved. But it is a different matter altogether to say that co-operation itself has come into existence as the end result of a process of evolution.

So co-operation cannot be explained simply as the (sometimes) necessary means to the ends of self-protection and self-advancement. Rather the forms of association in which we are involved with other people are part of what we are. Human existence cannot be described adequately in terms of separate existence.

That each person exists may be considered as a fact, in the singular. But however existence is described – in terms of actions, or in terms of ideas, feelings and motives, or in terms of biological processes and the influence of our genes – existence, each person's existence, consists of many facts. Existence is inescapably plural. Some of the facts of a particular organism's existence, as with a particular person's existence, are to do with that organism by itself, as with that person by himself/herself. Some are to do with that organism's connection to or interaction with other organisms, as some of the facts of a particular person's existence are to do with that person's connection to or interaction with other people.

Barbara Katz Rothman (1995) rejected what she described as the assumption that in the beginning there are individuals. She insisted on what she saw as the essential connectedness of existence as illustrated by pregnancy and childbirth: "We don't begin as separate beings ... we unfold from inside one another ... we are born connected. We are attached beings who learn to separate rather than separate beings who come together in certain circumstances." [91]

(It is interesting that Matt Ridley (1996) referred to atoms in order to define a supposed state of separate and self-interested existence, when he described the first life on earth as atomistic and individual.[92] He was not the first or only person to use the metaphor of the atom to represent separate, isolated existence and a lack of connection and interaction except at the most superficial level. For example, Norton Long (1986) described modern American cities as economic sites for combining and re-combining atoms.[93]

But atoms are not separate isolated entities which happen to meet up with each other on some occasions. An atom, as a fundamental unit of a particular chemical element, is a part of a whole: it is a sub-division. And atoms exist in a dynamic state: they move, they interact with each other; and they may combine to form molecules. If the atom is to be a metaphor for any state of existence it should be seen as a metaphor for connectedness, energy, interaction, association, bonding.)

REFERENCES

1. PLANT, Raymond (1974). *Community and ideology*. London: Routledge & Kegan Paul. p.15

2. HOBBES, Thomas. *Leviathan.* Harmondsworth: Pelican Classics, 1968. Pt.1, Chapt.1. p.161

3. HOBBES, Thomas. *Man and citizen: Thomas Hobbes' "De Homine" and "De Cive".* Edited by Bernard Gert. USA: Humanities; UK: Wheatsheaf, 1972 (repr.1978). p.110, footnote.

4. *ibid.* p.111

5. *ibid.* p.113

6. *ibid.* p.110, footnote

7. HOBBES, Thomas. *Leviathan.* Pt. I, Chapt. XIV. p.180

8. *ibid.* Pt. I, Chapt. XV. p.209

9. *ibid.* Pt. II, Chapt. XXI. p.262

10. GREEN, Karen. (1994). Christine de Pisan and Thomas Hobbes, *Philosophical Quarterly* (St. Andrews: Scots Philosophical Club and St. Andrews University). Vol.44, no.177. p.457

11. NOZICK, Robert. (1974). *Anarchy, state and utopia.* Oxford: Blackwell. Preface, p.ix

12. *ibid.* pp.169-170

13. *ibid.* p.33

14. AXELROD, Robert. (1984). *The evolution of co-operation.* New York: Basic Books. p.3

15. AXELROD, Robert, and HAMILTON, William D. (1984). The evolution of co-operation in biological systems, *The evolution of co-operation* (Chapter 5). p.89

16. TRIVERS, Robert L. (1971). The evolution of reciprocal altruism, *Quarterly Journal of Biology*. Vol.46 (March 1971). Reproduced in: *The sociobiology debate : readings on ethical and scientific issues.* Edited by Arthur L. Caplan. New York: Harper and Row. pp.214-215

17. AXELROD, Robert, COHEN, Michael D, and RIOLO, Rick L. (2001). Evolution of co-operation without reciprocity, *Nature* (London: Macmillan Magazines). Vol.414 (22 November 2001). pp.441-443

18. FEHR, Ernst, and GÄCHTER, Simon. (2002). Altruistic punishment in humans, *Nature* (London: Macmillan Magazines). Vol.415 (10 January 2002). pp.137-140

19. WILSON, Edward. (1978). *On human nature*. Cambridge, MS: Harvard University Press. p.13

20. BARKOW, Jerome H. (1992). Beneath new culture is old psychology, *The adapted mind : evolutionary psychology and the generation of culture*. Edited by Jerome H. Barkow, Leda Cosmides and John Tooby. New York; London: Oxford University Press. p.635

21. KITCHER, Philip. (1996). *The lives to come : the genetic revolution and human possibilities*. London: Allen Lane / Penguin. p.33

22. ROSE, Steven, with MILEUSNIC, Radmila. (1999). *The chemistry of life*. 4th ed. London: Penguin. p.39

23. KITCHER, Philip. *The lives to come*. p.31

24. ROSE, Steven. (1997). *Lifelines : biology, freedom, determinism*. p.158

25. *ibid.* p.38

26. RIDLEY, Mark. (1985). *The problems of evolution*. Oxford: Oxford University Press. p.148

27. GILBERT, Walter. (1992). A vision of the grail, *The code of codes : scientific and social issues in the Human Genome Project*. Edited by Daniel J. Kevles and Leroy Hoo. Cambridge, MS: Harvard University Press. pp.83-84

28. WATSON, James. (1990). The Human Genome Project : past, present and future, *Science* (Washington, DC: American Association for the Advancement of Science). Vol.248 (6th April 1990). p.44

29. DARWIN, Charles. (1859). *The origin of species by means of natural selection.* London: Penguin, 1985. p.115 (first edition: London: John Murray, 1859).

30. *ibid.* p.115

31. *ibid.* pp.116-117

32. *ibid.* p.119

33. DARWIN, Charles. (1857). Extract from an [edited] letter to Professor Asa Gray, Boston, USA, dated September 5th 1857. Quoted in, *Evolution.* Edited by Mark Ridley. Oxford: Oxford University Press, 1997. p.15

34. DARWIN, Charles. (1859). *The origin of species ...* p.115

35. *ibid.* p.444

36. MEDAWAR, P.B., and MEDAWAR, J.S. (1984). *Aristotle to Zoos : a philosophical dictionary of biology.* London: Weidenfeld & Nicolson. p.196

37. RIDLEY, Mark (ed.). (1997). *Evolution.* Oxford: Oxford University Press. p.10

38. BOWLER, Peter J. (1989). *The Mendelian revolution.* Baltimore, MD; John Hopkins University Press. pp.100-101

39. RIDLEY, Mark. (1985). *The problems of evolution.* Oxford: Oxford University Press. pp.16-18

40. *NEW Encyclopedia Britannica.* (1992). 15th edition. Macropedia. Vol.19. p.702

41. BOWLER, Peter J. (1989). *The Mendelian revolution.* pp.107-108

42. RIDLEY, Mark. (1985). *The problems of evolution.* p.152

43. PINKER, Steven. (1997). *How the mind works.* London: Allen Lane / Penguin. p.43

44. WILSON, Edward O. (1978). *On human nature.* Cambridge, MS: Harvard University Press. p.13

45. PINKER, Steven. (1997). *How the mind works.* p.20

46. BOUCHARD, Thomas J. (1997). Whenever the twain shall meet, *The Sciences* (New York: New York Academy of Sciences). Sept.-Oct. 1997. p.53

47. *ibid.* pp.53-54

48. GREENSPAN, Ralph. (1995). Understanding the genetic construction of behavior, *Scientific American* (New York: Scientific American Inc.). April 1995. pp.74-79

49. BOUCHARD, Thomas J. (1997). Whenever the twain shall meet. p.56

50. KITCHER, Philip. (1996). *The lives to come ...* p.60

51. *ibid.* p.99

52. LICHTENSTEIN. Paul ... [et al]. (2000). Environmental and heritable factors in the causation of cancer : analyses of cohorts of twins from Sweden, Denmark and Finland, *New England Journal of Medicine.* Vol.343, no.2 (13th July 2000). pp.78-85

53. HOBBES, Thomas. *Leviathan.* Pt. I, Chapt. V. p.209

54. RIDLEY, Matt. (1996). *The origins of virtue : human instincts and the evolution of co-operation.* Harmondsworth: Penguin / Viking. p.252

55. *ibid.* p.252

56. WILSON, Edward O. (1975). *Sociobiology : the new synthesis.* Cambridge, MS: Belknap Press ; Harvard University Press. pp.3, 118

57. TRIVERS, Robert L. (1971). The evolution of reciprocal altruism. pp.214-215

58. AXELROD, Robert, and HAMILTON, William D. (1984). The evolution of co-operation in biological systems. pp.88-89

59. AXELROD, Robert, COHEN, Michael D, and RIOLO, Rick L. (2001). Evolution of co-operation without reciprocation. pp.441-443

60. FEHR, Ernst, and GÄCHTER, Simon. (2002). Altruistic punishment in humans. pp.137-140

61. RIDLEY, Matt. (1996). *The origins of virtue.* p.14

62. AXELROD, Robert. (1984). *The evolution of co-operation.*

63. COVENEY, Peter, and HIGHFIELD, Roger. (1995). *Frontiers of complexity : the search for order in a chaotic world.* London: Faber & Faber. p.223

64. COSMIDES, Leda, and TOOBY, John. (1992). Cognitive adaptations to social exchange, *The adapted mind : evolutionary psychology and the generation of culture.* Edited by Jerome H. Barkow, Leda Cosmides and John Tooby. New York; London: Oxford University Press. pp.164, 167

65. BOESCH, Christopher, and WHITEN, Andrew. (2001). The culture of chimpanzees, *Scientific American* (New York: Scientific American Inc.). January 2001. pp.49-56

66. *ibid.* p.55

67. KUPER, Adam. (1994). *The chosen primate : human nature and cultural diversity.* Cambridge, MS: Harvard University Press. pp.74, 92

68. MAY, Robert, NOWAK, Martin, and SIGMUND, Karl. (1995). The arithmetic of mutual help, *Scientific American* (New York: Scientific American Inc.). June 1995. p.55

69. KAISER, Dale, and LOSICK, Richard. (1997). Why and how bacteria communicate, *Scientific American* (New York: Scientific American Inc.). February 1997. pp.52-57

70. KROOS, Lee, LENSKI, Richard, and VELICER, Gregory. (2000). Developmental cheating in the social bacterium Myxococcus Xanthus, *Nature* (London: Macmillan Magazines). Vol.404, no.6778 (6th April 2000). pp.598-600

71. TRIVERS, Robert L. (1985). *Social evolution.* Menlo Park, CA: Benjamin-Carnegie. p.386

72. RIDLEY, Matt. (1996). *The origins of virtue.* p.6

73. *ibid.* pp.41-44

74. KUPER, Adam. (1994). *The chosen primate.* pp.215-216

75. *ibid.* pp.215-216

76. RIDLEY, Matt. (1996). *The origins of virtue.* p.152

77. *ibid.* p.188

78. BULMER, Martin. (1986). *Neighbours : the work of Philip Abrams.* Cambridge: Cambridge University Press. p.115

79. WILSON, Edward O. (1990). Interview, *The Guardian* (London). 24th August 1990. p.17

80. RIDLEY, Matt. (1996). *The origins of virtue.* p.20

81. POPPER, Karl. (1976). *Unended quest : an intellectual biography.* Glasgow: Collins / Fontana. pp.193-194

82. MIDGLEY, Mary. (1994). *The ethical primate.* London: Routledge. p.3

83 (a). SCHWARTZ, Barry. (1993). Why altruism is impossible ... and ubiquitous, *Social Service Review* (Chicago, ILL: University of Chicago Press). Vol.67, no.3 (September 1993). pp.313-343

83 (b). *ibid.* pp.316-317

84. MIDGLEY, Mary. (1994). *The ethical primate.* p.141

85. *ibid.* p.142

86. GALLESE, Vittorio, and GOLDMAN, Alvin. (1998). Mirror neurons and the simulation theory of mind reading, *Trends in Cognitive Science.* Vol.2, Issue 12 (1st December 1998). pp.493-501

87. RAMACHANDRAN, V.S. (2000). Mirror neurons and imitation learning as the driving force behind 'The Great Leap Forward' in human evolution, *Edge.* No.69 (June 2000). pp.4-9

88. RIDLEY, Matt. (1996). *The origins of virtue.* p.188

89. NOZICK, Robert. (1974). *Anarchy, state and utopia.* p.33

90. MAYNARD SMITH, John. (2000). Quoted in: A tale of two selves, *Science* (Washington, DC: American Association for the Advancement of Science). Vol.290 (3rd November 2000). pp.949-950

91. ROTHMAN, Barbara Katz. (1995). Of maps and imaginations : sociology confronts the genome, *Social Problems* (Berkeley, CA: University of California Press). Vol.42, no.1 (February 1995). p.4

92. RIDLEY, Matt. (1996). *The origins of virtue.* p.152

93. LONG, Norton. (1986). The city as a political community, *Journal of Community Psychology* (Brandon, VT: Clinical Psychology Publishing Corp.). Vol.14, no.1. p.72

5

LOCALITY AND COMMUNITY : ARE COMMUNITIES THERE?

Is there an association between community and place? - Assumptions about community and place – Community, movement and change – Is there a link between community and place or community and space? - How important are definitions?

Community is where community happens

Martin Buber, *Between Man and Man*

Is there an association between community and place?

In the last chapter I examined two quite different ways of looking at our social experience that reflected two quite different views of human nature: that we are individualist creatures, and forms of association with other people are no more than necessary arrangements to protect and advance our individual self-interests; or that we are social creatures, and forms of association with other people help to express what and who we are.

It seemed to me that an individualist view of human nature may depend on a presumption of original solitude: that in the beginning there were only individual people. I argued that there was no evidence for any stage of human evolution which corresponded with such a picture of human existence; and that there was sufficient evidence to suggest that cooperation has been fundamental to existence from the earliest and most elementary life forms to present times and the most complex life forms. So it did not seem to be reasonable to seek to explain cooperation and cooperative habits only in terms of self interest and self advancement through mutual advantage.

I would conclude, therefore, that community can be an appropriate idea to apply to our social experience, and that it may be realistic to talk about community in relation to forms of association between people. However, that does not prove that a particular application of the idea of community is valid. If, for example, I describe a particular group of people as a community then in effect I am making a statement about their relationships with each other. But does the actual state of their relationships justify that statement? If I describe a group of people who are living in a particular place as the community of (X), I am making a statement about their relationships with each other and I am linking those relationships to the place in which they are living. I am making a direct association between community and place. But is there a direct association?

Often the association between community and place is made uncritically and reflects a series of assumptions about how and where people live, and what the significance is of where they live. For example, there is the assumption that living in a particular place involves people in groups or organisations or institutions which are associated with that place; and there is the assumption that relationships will develop simply on the basis of place and type of residence (see Chapters 1 and 3 above). And not only are people supposed to live in 'the community' or in the 'local community'. Most people, it is supposed, live in particular local communities. Even Robert Nozick, who insisted in *Anarchy, State and Utopia* (1974) that there were only different individual people with their own individual lives, declared that we live in particular communities.[1]

To talk about 'the community' or 'a community' suggests a particular group of people, *i.e.* a group of people who are distinct from other people who do not belong to that group, although those other people are likely to belong to other groups. To talk about a local community suggests a group of people who are distinct from other people not only because those other people do not belong to their group, but also because those other people live in another place. So a 'local community' can be seen as an actual social unit which is characterised by physical limits or boundaries. It is characterised also by social limits: some people belong and others outside its boundaries, do not.

Those who belong are involved in various forms of association with each other. The *Blackwell Dictionary of 20th Century Social Thought* considered that at a minimum, the word community referred to a group of people who were identified by geographical boundaries, shared institutions and interaction.[2]

Often there seems to be an instinctive assumption that locality or physical proximity in themselves may give a special quality to or may extend or deepen relationships. There is a related assumption that people who live beside or near to each other will form an identifiable group with common institutions and informal networks. These assumptions are demonstrated in the Cumberledge Report of 1986 which reviewed the community nursing service in England and Wales. It believed that nursing services – including district nurses, health visitors and school nurses – should be organised locally; and it recommended the development of a neighbourhood nursing service which could relate to "... the informal networks of support which grew up in any community." [3]

A further assumption which underlies these assumptions is that communities are real: they are there. The *Blackwell Dictionary of 20th Century Thought* (1983) insisted on the continuing importance of community as a reality in most people's lives. The *Making Belfast Work Strategy Statement* of March 1995 referred to local communities, communities in decline and community infrastructure and spoke for communities having a real say in policies which affected their daily lives (see Chapter 3). Gerald D. Suttles in *The Social Construction of Communities* (1974) saw an historical dimension to the reality of community in most people's lives. He declared that there was evidence that local communities (in the USA) had varied enormously in their stability and autonomy over the previous two hundred years.[4] Peter Barclay (1982) demonstrated a belief amounting to a kind of faith when he declared that we all know that community is there. [5]

This assumption that communities are real, that they are there, is reflected also in the belief that people belong to particular communities whatever the actual state of their relationships. Eric Emerson and Chris Hatton (1994) in their review of research on the relocation of learning disabled people from hospital to community, concluded that the users of community-based services lacked "real presence in their communities" and had not developed their participation in "their surrounding community".[6] (But if anyone lacks real presence in or does not participate in 'their community', then why describe it as 'their community'?)

Assumptions about community and place

If communities are real, if they are there; if people live in particular communities, in particular places – then each community should occupy a different space, and it should be possible to describe something of each person's identity and self on the basis of where he/she lives and who lives beside him/her and who lives further away.

But the complexity of actual social existence calls into question the above assumptions and the direct association between the idea of community and place which underlies them. For example: people living side by side in the same place may identify with different institutions, forms of association or networks: with different 'communities'. Furthermore, people may be simultaneously neighbours and strangers. Rosemary Harris (1972), in her study of a town in Northern Ireland observed how members of different groups within the town could have apparently close relations while remaining essentially separate.[7] Graham Day and Jonathan Murdoch (1993), in their study of the Ithon Valley in Mid-Wales, noted that farming and farming families were central to the local institutions and networks of the valley and had long standing attachments to the place because farming was a core economic activity. However, although 'place' might help to describe one aspect of farming families' relationships and their positions in the valley, it was largely irrelevant to relationships derived from economic activity. Individual farms were tied to quite different markets. Farmers in the valley were part of a network of relationships which stretched across Mid-Wales.[8]

And people living in the same place do not necessarily experience the same community as each other. In their review of community and locality studies, Graham Crow and Graham Allan (1994) observed that people living in the same area could experience that area differently.[9] Jocelyn Cornwell, in her study of health and illness in East London (1984), noted radical differences in the way people experienced community. These differences in experiencing community were especially striking when they were between men and women living in the same households. She described the case of Mick and Sarah, who did not experience the same community as each other: they occupied different spaces, socially as well as geographically. In general, Jocelyn Cornwell considered that women occupied a much wider range of common spaces than men.[10] R. Wright (1989) studied the impact of long term migrations into and 'gentrification' of Stoke Newington in London. A consequence of this process, he believed, was that people lived in different worlds even though they shared the same place of residence.[11]

It is not necessary to share the same space in order to share experiences. Pierrette Hondagneu-Sotelo (1994) described how Mexican immigrant women organised their response to paid domestic labour, cleaning private homes in a part of California. The women did not share the same working space. Usually they worked alone in different houses and negotiated their terms and conditions of work on a one-to-one basis with each individual householder. But the solitary nature of their work and their negotiations with their employers contrasted with the strength of the network they developed between each other. In various social settings, the women met and exchanged experiences and tips on how to do jobs or negotiate with employers, or combine several different jobs at the same time, or cope with work-related ailments.[12]

Community, movement and change

The movement of people from one place to another, as in migration, calls into question a direct association between locality or place and community, and assumptions that people live in particular communities in particular places. Such assumptions imply that if people move from a place with which a 'local community' is identified, then either they remain members of that community although not in the same place; or they cease to be members: they cease to belong. But people's identities – who they are and how they see themselves – are not fixed entities which either they bring with them intact or hand in when they move. Nor is the place, the local community which they leave a fixed entity which remains as it is when they leave and when or if they return. Katy Gardner (1995), in her study of patterns of migration from and continuing ties with a village in the Sylhet area of North East Bangladesh, concluded that migration involved a constant process of re-invention – "... as we physically move so too do our personal and social boundaries shift ..." [13] She described the case of Abdullah Meer, who returned regularly to his home village, but who found that there were less people there each time whom he knew. He had left a place, but when he returned to that place, the people – or 'the community' – whom he met were not simply those whom he had left.

The Scottish Gaelic poet Domhnall MacAmhlaigh (Donald MacAulay) described the same process in his poem 'Comharra stiùiridh' ('Landmark'). A native of the island of Bernera off Lewis in the Outer Hebrides, he spent his working life away from the island, but he returned each year – a "yearly pilgrim". But the island/community he found on his return visits became less and less the island/community which he held in his mind. That island/community remained in his consciousness as a landmark in his life elsewhere:

And that is not my island;
it submerged long ago ...
and the part that submerged in me of it,
sun-bower and iceberg,
sails the ocean I travel,
a primary landmark
dangerous, essential, demanding.

(English translation by the author) [14]

Forms of association may develop between people who do not occupy the same space and who live at great distances from each other. Martin Woollacott (1994) commented on the emergence of what he described as modern diasporas: "... international, intercontinental communities of particular ethnic or religious origin." He suggested that often what were supposed to be minorities within particular countries were in fact "elements in global communities that have separate international lives of their own." Their distinguishing mark was the ease with which they could maintain a degree of separateness and a separate cultural identity. In this they were aided by modern means of transport, especially air travel, and by modern means of communication.[15]

Perhaps for people who see themselves as belonging to such an 'international, intercontinental' community, locality and a sense of place are irrelevant to their common institutions and their relationships and forms of association with each other. Certainly their community is not there, in the sense that it is not bounded by or defined by a particular place.

Is there a link between community and place or community and space?

Place or physical space or distance may not in themselves determine the dimensions, the relationships, the character of community. So is there an association between physical space and relationships, or an association between physical space and community; and if so, what are they? I would suggest that the association of locality with community can be misleading. The relevance of place or space to community is not in boundaries which are supposed to enclose a particular group of people or indicate limits on a kind of group membership which depends on living in one place rather than another. Such ways of thinking about people and their relationships and forms of association with each other can distort the reality of social existence.

The relevance of place or space to community, I would suggest, is in the way in which they influence social existence.

Community is a process rather than a place. As a process it derives from interaction between people and the relationships, forms of association and institutions which grow from those interactions. People encounter each other in space and time. Physical proximity or distance influence the number of encounters and the frequency of interaction between people. Increasingly, people recognise and respond to sympathetic others, and enter into forms of association with others.

The 'modern diaspora' described by Martin Woollacott (see above) can be viewed as a community which exists across international boundaries. The relationships and forms of association and common institutions which characterise this community do not depend for their existence on a particular space. However, they do not emerge in a void. It is unlikely that they will emerge without reference to place or space or distance. Such an international community, which crosses continents, is likely to draw on and develop from previous family and kin ties and a consciousness of shared beliefs and traditions. Possibly it may refer back to home areas or settlements which people or the generations before them have left.

Peter Willmott, in his analysis of neighbourhood and community (1986) reviewed research into social ties and noted that the majority of people surveyed had relations with people living nearby.[16] Mark La Gory and John Pipkin (1981) pointed out that a tremendous number of studies on the effects of physical proximity or distance on human interaction led to the conclusion that interaction decreased as distance increased.[17] In this context they quoted George Kingsley Zipf (1949) and his 'principle of least effort' which argued that the shorter a distance one has to travel to perform a certain activity, the more likely it is that the activity will be performed. They concluded that "distance moulds social interaction."

Mark La Gory and John Pipkin appeared to claim a simple and direct association between proximity or distance and social ties. I would suggest that the association is more subtle and indirect. Proximity/distance influences not only the frequency of interaction, but the frequency of particular kinds or particular qualities of interaction. The evidence on which Mark La Gory and John Pipkin relied suggests that we will meet proportionately more people from the area near to us than from areas further away. But the more people we meet from a given area, and the more often we meet the same people, then the more scope there will be for those exchanges which indicate shared concerns, interests and sympathies. The more likely it is that we will meet people with whom we can and do form bonds. Peter Willmott (1986) observed a dimension of time as well as of space in influencing the frequency and outcomes of social interactions. Research led him to the conclusion that length of residence was likely to affect social networks and community sense rather than urban scale or population density.[18] Mike Savage and Alan Warde, in their survey of urban culture (1993), considered that repeated interactions encouraged more intense interpersonal sentiments, whether of belonging or antagonism.[19]

What is important, I would suggest, is not space or proximity/distance in themselves, but the process of encounter; of interaction; of relationships which may develop and sometimes do. Space and proximity/distance facilitate but do not determine or mould social interaction. Space does not enclose or bound relationships. Space offers opportunities for interaction, as for the development of economic activity. Marilyn Gray and Andrea Bernstein (1994) illustrated this relevance of space to community in their description of the situation of a group of women and children who were living in shacks on the pavement in the centre of the city of Durban in South Africa.[20] The women had come to the city from impoverished rural areas looking both for shelter and opportunities to earn some money for themselves and their families. They settled in an area of vacant land in the city centre known to the authorities as Block AK. Their main economic activity was collecting, buying and re-selling old plastic containers, which were important in low income areas for the transport and storage of water. They established themselves so successfully that in time the authorities gave legal recognition to their trading activities by issuing licences.

Marilyn Gray and Andrea Bernstein observed how the women functioned as a community. They did not compete on price among themselves. They gave each other mutual aid and support: for example, established residents advised newcomers how to adapt. They shared skills and resources. Some of the women practised hairdressing to add to their income, but they did not charge fellow residents for the service. And the women acted together to negotiate with the authorities to obtain trading licences.

The women, it would seem, were attracted to Block AK because it was vacant. Also it lay beside the main railway station in Durban, which brought substantial passing trade. The space of Block AK provided opportunities for shelter and for activities which could earn some money for the women. It was also the space within which (for the most part) they interacted and cooperated with each other.

The arguments above may lead to the conclusion that there is no such thing as local community or a local community, if by the term we mean a group of people who are resident in a particular place and who are involved in a network of relationships with each other and in common forms of association and common institutions. 'Local community' implies that those relationships, forms of association and institutions are enclosed or bounded by the place. It implies a direct association between community and place; but the reality of our social experience is that it is more complex and more open-ended.

How important are definitions?

On the other hand, it could be argued that this is an unnecessarily strict approach to the use of a word. It could be argued that at certain times it is convenient to use 'community' as a kind of shorthand, to indicate that a group of people have something in common. 'Local community' could be used as a kind of shorthand to indicate simply that people live beside each other in a particular place, and that it is convenient up to a point to observe those people as being together, as having common concerns and interests. 'Local community' could be used as a simple term, pragmatically and cautiously, without making large claims about social relationships and networks and organisations.

The problem with this approach is that few words in the English language are used more incautiously than 'community'. Firstly, it is used as are few other words to express values. Raymond Williams in *Keywords* (1983) observed its use as a "warmly persuasive word" and noted that it seemed never to be used unfavourably.[21] Secondly, it and 'local community' are used as are few other words or terms without explanation or discussion. Often the use of 'community' and of 'local community' seem to carry whole eco-systems of assumption.

REFERENCES

1. NOZICK, Robert. (1974). *Anarchy, state and utopia.* Oxford: Blackwell. p.332
2. *BLACKWELL dictionary of 20th century social thought.* Oxford: Blackwell. 'Community', p.98
3. CUMBERLEDGE, Julia. (1986). Neighbourhood nursing : a force for care, *Report of the Community Nursing Review.* London: HMSO. p.16
4. SUTTLES, Gerald D. (1972). *The social construction of communities.* Chicago: University of Chicago Press. p.9
5. BARCLAY Committee. (1982). *Social workers : their roles and tasks.* London: Bedford Square Press. para.13.24
6. EMERSON, Eric, and HATTON, Chris. (1994). *Moving out : relocation from hospital to community.* London: HMSO. Introduction, p.iii
7. HARRIS, Rosemary. (1972). Introduction, *Prejudice and tolerance in Ulster : a study of neighbours and strangers in a border community.* Manchester: Manchester University Press
8. DAY, Graham, and MURDOCH, Jonathan. (1993). Locality and community : coming to terms with place, *Sociological Review* (London: Routledge & Kegan Paul). Vol.41, no.1. p.96
9. ALLAN, Graham, and CROW, Graham. (1994). *Community life : an introduction to local social relations.* Hemel Hempstead: Harvester Wheatsheaf. p.157

10. CORNWELL, Jocelyn. (1984). *Hard-earned lives : accounts of health and illness from East London.* London: Tavistock. p.50

11. WRIGHT, R. (1989). The ghosting of the inner city, *Divided nation : social and cultural change in Britain.* Edited by L. McDonnell, P. Sarré and C. Hammett. London: Hodder & Stoughton. pp.282-3

12. HONDAGNEU-SOTELO, Pierrette. (1994). Regulating the unregulated : domestic workers' social networks, *Social Problems* (Berkeley, CA: University of California Press). Vol.41, no.1. pp.50-64

13. GARDNER, Katy. (1995). *Global migrants, local lives : travel and transformation in rural Bangladesh.* Oxford: OUP. p.vii, p.1

14. MACAMHLAIGH, Domhnall. (1967). Comharra stiùiridh, *Seòbhrach as a'chlaich.* Glasgow: Gairm. pp.35, 92

15. WOOLLACOTT, Martin. (1994). When brotherhood transcends borders, *Guardian* (London). 10th August 1994. p.18

16. WILLMOTT, Peter. (1986). *Social networks : informal care and public policy.* London: Policy Studies Institute. p.89

17. LA GORY, Mark, and PIPKIN, John. (1981). *Urban social space.* Belmont, CA: Wandsworth. p.25

18. WILLMOTT, Peter. (1986). *Social networks : informal care and public policy.* p.89

19. SAVAGE, Mike, and WARDE, Alan. (1993). Perspectives on urban culture, *Urban sociology, capitalism and modernity.* London: Macmillan. pp.96-121. Quoted in: *Sociology of urban communities.* Edited by Michael Harloe. Vol.1. Cheltenham: Elgar, 1996. p.329 [1]

20. BERNSTEIN, Andrea, and GRAY, Marilyn. (1994). Pavement people and informal communities, *International Social Work* (London: Sage). Vol.37. pp.149-163

21. WILLIAMS, Raymond. (1983). *Keywords.* London: Fontana Paperbacks / Flamingo. p.76

[1] 2nd ed. of *Urban sociology, capitalism and modernity* published by Palgrave Macmillan, November 2002

Part 3:

The dimensions and the limits of community

6

IS THERE A COMMUNITY WHICH CARES?

Caring without community? – Caring and relationships – Caring, different kinds of help, and what people want for themselves – Conclusion: is there an association between community and caring?

Caring without community?

Community, or 'the community', has been seen by many as a vital component of community care. Julia Twigg and Karl Atkin in *Carers Perceived* (1994) observed that care in the community had been a dominant theme of UK government policies since the 1960s.[1] The Seebohm Report on the personal social services in England and Wales (1968) presented the community as both the provider and the recipient of services.[2] The Barclay Report on the roles and tasks of social workers (1982) perceived an important feature of community to be the capacity of networks of people within it to mobilise individual and collective responses to adversity.[3] The Griffiths Report on community care (1988) sought to place responsibility for care with 'the local community'.[4] In *Towards Caring Communities : Community Development and Community Care* (1997) Alan Barr, Jack Drysdale and Paul Henderson advocated "active engagement with communities" for the development of community care services. They referred to the potential networks of support for service users in service users' own neighbourhoods.[5]

I would suggest that community implies some degree or form of association and some common bond. It implies public and social as compared to private and personal. Community care, or caring activities which go by the name of community, might be taken to imply at least some of these elements of community in relation to activities for the support and care of dependent people.

But there is a considerable body of evidence which points to the conclusion that care for dependent people, outside of the (minority) role of public and private agencies and professional workers, is essentially personal and private and often isolating; that most often it is provided by family members rather than by neighbours and friends; and that most often it is provided by one particular person in the family, who, more often than not, is a woman.

From their study of carers, Julia Twigg and Karl Atkin concluded that restrictiveness as they described it was central to the lives of most carers. Various factors restricted the lives of carers: the need to do things for the cared-for person, to be with them; and also a general anxiety about what might happen in their absence.[6] Many carers found that caring eroded their social networks, and many experienced difficulty in maintaining close relationships.[7] Often a carer relied upon the cared-for person for company and opportunities for a social life.[8] Some people caring for their own spouses did not want to pursue and independent social life: they wished to be able to engage in social relations together with their cared-for spouse rather than apart from them.[9]

The amount of time spent in looking after the cared-for person can consume much of the carer's week. Sharon Haffenden, in a study for the Social Services Inspectorate of the Department of Health (1991), reported that 45% of carers looking after someone in the same household devoted at least fifty hours per week to the care of that person.[10] In Northern Ireland a survey by Eileen Evason and Dorothy Whittington for the Equal Opportunities Commission (1995) found that for the majority of carers interviewed, caring added up to more than a full time job.[11]

Caring is likely to cost the carer in terms of employment prospects, and therefore in terms of income. Caroline Glendinning (1992) concluded from her study that giving help and support to a severely disabled or frail elderly person invariably had an adverse effect on the carer's participation in the labour market.[12] Gillian Parker, in her review of research on informal care (1990), noted that carers of elderly, non-elderly and children alike are often forced to give up work, or lose time if they continue in paid employment, in order to continue caring.[13] In *Caring on the Breadline* (2000), a report of a survey of the experience of members of the Carers' National Association, Emily Holzhausen and Vicky Pearlman observed that seven out of ten carers under the age of fifty years and eight out of ten carers under the age of sixty years had given up work in order to continue caring.[14] Karl Atkin and Janet Rollings (1996) observed that racial inequalities in income, employment and housing might accentuate the material costs and difficulties of caring.[15]

Usually support for the cared-for person comes from someone in the same household, rather than from individuals or groups from outside. Audrey Hunt, in her analysis of the General Household Survey (1978), observed that for older people unable to perform various tasks without help, much the greater part of that help came from another person in the same household.[16] In their study in Northern Ireland, Eileen Evason and Dorothy Whittington (1995) observed that most carers lived in the same household as the person for whom they cared.[17] Gillian Parker, from her review of research into caring (1990), insisted that 'care by the community' almost always meant care by family members, with little support from others in 'the community'. Furthermore, caring tasks were not shared equally between family members: once one person in the family had been identified as the main carer, other family members or relatives withdrew, although this pattern varied between dependency groups.[18] Karl Atkin and Janet Rollings (1996) reported similar patterns among Asian and Afro-Caribbean families in Britain.[19]

Anna Briggs and Judith Oliver (1985), in their compilation of the views of carers, reported that the carers were sick of hearing about community care which often, as far as they were concerned, meant themselves single-handed.[20] Indeed, official policy or practice may increase the isolation of carers. Gillian Parker and Dot Lawson (1994) concluded that overall, the provision of services had been biased both against those whose carers lived in the same household as themselves, and those whose carers were related to them.[21]

Clearly the evidence above could be interpreted to suggest that caring for dependent or disabled people is usually private and isolating as well as being personal. Families, and individual members of families, are seen to be left to care on their own for adults and children. It may be concluded that there is no community which provides or offers assistance.

Caring and relationships

But such a conclusion – that there is no community which provides or offers assistance - does not reflect the reality of what people want for themselves and for their relationships with each other. Julia Twigg and Karl Atkin, in their study of carers (1994), affirmed that caring took place within relationships and that the cared-for person was as important as the carer.[22] Evidence suggested that acceptance of the caring role, of giving help to the cared-for person, could and did reflect the wishes of the person giving help. Usually acceptance of the caring role reflected what people chose for themselves, rather than the pressures of cultural standards or of social structures.

That is not to say that people who accept a caring role do not wish for more support, or do not resent their isolation and their difficulties in maintaining and finding employment. But their difficulties, or their resentment or their wish or demand for more support does not mean that they wish to relinquish their caring roles. Eileen Evason and Dorothy Whittington, in their study of caring (1995), noted that only one person from all whom they interviewed appeared to have taken on the caring role reluctantly.[23] Mike Fisher, in his review of research (1994) observed a willing acceptance of the caring role. Many carers asserted that they chose to care – "they would have it no other way."[24] Clare Wenger, in her study of help and helping networks in North Wales (1992), found that most carers had a good relationship with the persons for whom they cared, and that they resisted giving up their caring role.[25] Melanie Henwood, in a report for the Carers National Association (1998), found that most people who were providing care wished to continue to do so, although they complained of lack of support from the National Health Service.[26]

Often the caring role, and who undertakes it, reflects existing relationships. This is true especially of older carers and older spouses who undertake a caring role. Clare Wenger (1992) found that most people caring for older people were themselves middle aged or older: either the cared-for persons' spouses or women relatives in their late fifties and sixties.[27] Mike Fisher (1994) reported on research which indicated that the major part of care of older people was provided by other older people. Care by spouses predominated when the cared-for person was severely disabled.[28] He drew attention also to studies on men caring for their spouses who discussed their role in terms of a sense of love and duty, and a desire to pay back for the care received from their wives.[29]

Caring, different kinds of help and what people want for themselves

How care is defined and who gives care are questions which are related to ideas about who needs help and for what purposes they need help. Care or 'informal care' is interpreted often to refer to providing the help which some people need for the basic tasks of everyday living: tasks which they cannot carry out at all themselves or cannot carry out without help. This is precisely the kind of care, the kind of help, which is the most personal and possibly the most intimate, and which depends more than any other on the familiarity and trust of previously existing relationships. Thus Julia Twigg and Karl Atkin (1994) could assert that caring was embedded in relationships of obligation such as marriage, parenthood or kinship.[30]

It is too easy to use the terms 'care', 'caring' and 'carers' when in fact we are referring to certain kinds of help and certain kinds of situations in which people may need help – and then conclude that if friends, or neighbours or 'the community' are not involved in those situations it may well be so because they are uncaring.

In fact, just as evidence suggests that acceptance of the caring role, of giving help to the cared-for person, can and does reflect the wishes of the person giving help; so also evidence suggests that receiving help can and does reflect the wishes of the cared-for person. What users of services, the recipients of care, want for themselves and what they expect from different groups of people, are vital factors in determining whether family or kin or 'the community' (friends, neighbours and others) offer help. Clare Wenger, in her review of literature on helping networks (1992), noted that people turned to family more frequently for help with sickness and less for companionship; and were more likely to turn to friends and neighbours for companionship.[31] Martin Bulmer, in his account of the work of Philip Abrams and his team on neighbours and neighbouring (1986), reported that "... respect for privacy was consistently identified in studies as an enormously valued component of positive neighbouring."[32]

A survey among older people in the Exeter area in 1988, as part of a linked group of research projects in five European countries, found that friends and neighbours accounted for the majority of visits to the home. But the frequency of contacts did not indicate their intensity or significance. Friends and neighbours could "keep an eye on things" and give "small but significant daily kindnesses and services." However, at critical moments – such as illness or death – the friends and neighbours retired discreetly and the family took over.[33]

This was illustrated in Clare Wenger's study of support networks for older people in rural areas of North Wales. The study was based on a series of interviews in 1979, with an in-depth survey of thirty selected people between 1983 and 1987, and follow-up interviews in 1987 with the people interviewed in 1979 who were still living. Clare Wenger observed that the people who were interviewed expected different things from different kinds of relationship. She identified a hierarchy of expectations which people had in relation to the help and support which they might expect from each kind of person and each kind of relationship. The greatest level of expectation was from spouses, followed by adult children. Only these two groups were considered for support requiring intimacy or privacy, as with personal, nursing care or assistance in financial matters. Following them were friends, to whom the older people would look for companionship and expressive support; and neighbours, to whom they would look for practical and emergency support.[34]

Mike Fisher (1994) cast some doubt on the understanding of family obligations which is expressed in the idea of a hierarchy of expectations; especially in the relation to the sense of obligation to care for spouses. He asked whether this understanding of family obligations – being derived as he saw it from the study of white, western, majority culture families – might be less applicable within minority ethnic groups and quoted a number of studies which suggested this.[35] But if the particular model of the hierarchy of expectations which Clare Wenger describes is less applicable within other ethnic groups or cultural traditions, then another model of the hierarchy of expectations as to who will provide what kind of help and support may be applicable. Waqar I.U. Ahmad, in a survey of research on family obligations among Asian communities in Britain (1996), noted similar hierarchies of expectation. One difference as to how this was expressed was in a reliance on sons and daughters-in-law, rather than daughters to provide help and support to aged parents.[36]

The expectations of the cared-for person as to who will give help and support, and the sense of obligation – and the commitment – of the person giving help and support may follow different forms in different settings and relationships. But again the idea of a hierarchy of expectations may remain valid. In Cherrill Hicks' study of who looked after people at home (1988), Kevin Brompton described caring for his partner Alan, who died of AIDS, in Alan's last year. He had very supportive friends and in the last months of Alan's life a rota of friends with house keys would call in with Alan when Kevin was at work. Kevin himself organised all the lotions and ointments which Alan needed and he bathed Alan when he was in hospital. He looked after Alan, as Alan knew he would.[37]

Care can be exercised by one person for another through supportive networks without the first person intervening directly with the second person. Caring for someone, in the fundamental sense, means being concerned about the wellbeing of someone of whom you have some knowledge and having the intention to give support to that person and when necessary, taking some action to give support to that person. It does not mean necessarily having direct contact with the cared-for person. Rosanne Cecil, John Offer and Fred St. Leger, in their study of informal care in the town of Glengow in Northern Ireland (1987), compared the attitudes of social workers, who were not based in the town, and who were not a familiar sight to the people of Glengow, to the attitudes of police officers who were based in the town and who were a familiar sight. The social workers believed that Glengow was "not very neighbourly" and "not a particularly caring community." The police sergeant considered that people were friendly towards each other and there were no instances of people being neglected. If, for example, neighbours knew of old people being in difficulty they would help directly or tell the police.[38]

Conclusion: is there an association between community and caring?

Caring for others – in the fundamental sense of being concerned for the welfare of other persons of whom we have some knowledge, with the intention to help if necessary, and taking appropriate action to help – may be expressed as collective action. It may be expressed as an organised group process or as a self-help group activity. But caring for others is as likely to be expressed on a smaller, more personal scale. And when caring for other persons means regular help with some or other of the basic tasks of everyday living, it is likely to be an essentially private as well as personal function and to be based on pre-existing relationships.

Caring for other persons reflects broadly the choices and expectations of the persons giving help and receiving help, rather than any rejection by friends, neighbours or 'community'. However, it may serve to restrict the other relationships of the person giving help, and even to isolate her or him. There is no evidence that anyone chooses or seeks such restrictions or isolation. People who care for others and who help them with basic everyday tasks may wish for more support for their helping role, and they may complain of lack of resources, but that does not mean that they would reject their helping role when they are able to do so.

This kind of personal, often private and sometimes isolating caring role does not prove that 'community' is a myth. It proves that community goes only so far, that it may be relevant to some caring/helping situations but not to others. That this should be so is not because supposed traditional, all-inclusive communities or neighbourhoods have withered away. It is so because it is in the nature of some of our relationships with each other. 'Community' can refer to our relationships and forms of association with other people. It can express a dimension of our social existence – but not all dimensions. There is a dimension of our relations with other people which is outside the scope of community because those relations are too small-scale or personal or private to justify the use of the term 'community'; even if the scope of this personal, private dimension may vary between different periods of time or different societies.

But it seems that many people find it difficult not to imagine that once upon a time there were communities or neighbourhoods that included all or most of the relationships of all or most of the people who resided within them; and that these communities/neighbourhoods have since declined or fragmented or disappeared. Something of this way of thinking can be seen in the concept of the community of limited liability which was advanced by M. Janowitz (1952) [39] and A.H. Hunter and G.D. Suttles (1972) [40] and quoted by Martin Bulmer in his analysis of community care (1987). The community of limited liability was seen as "a mosaic of partially overlapping, locally based activities, groups and administrative areas." [41] The citizens' participation in more than one community of limited liability meant that their loyalties, interests and demands were fragmented. But all the forms of association between people to which we might refer to as communities are of limited liability in the sense that none of them imply the unlimited liability of people living within them or identified with them for the problems and needs of all the others living within them.

Community can represent one dimension of our social existence, of our relations with other people. Usually the absence of a 'community dimension' in particular helping situations does not demonstrate an absence of community or the collapse of communities, but merely the limits to the relevance of the idea community.

REFERENCES

1. ATKIN, Karl, and TWIGG, Julia. (1994). *Carers perceived.* Buckingham: Open University Press. p.3
2. *REPORT of the Committee on Local Authority and Allied Personal Services* [Seebohm Report] (1968). London: HMSO
3. BARCLAY Committee. (1982). *Social workers : their roles and tasks.* London: Bedford Square Press
4. GRIFFITHS, Roy (Chairman). (1988). *Community care : agenda for action.* London: HMSO
5. BARR, Alan, DRYSDALE, Jack, and HENDERSON, Paul. (1997). *Towards caring communities : community development and community care.* Brighton: Pavilion. p.vii
6. ATKIN, Karl, and TWIGG, Julia. (1994). *Carers perceived.* p.36
7. *ibid.* p.41
8. *ibid.* p.36
9. *ibid.* p.38
10. HAFFENDEN, Sharon. (1991). *Getting it right for carers.* London: HMSO for the Department of Health. p.140
11. EVASON, Eileen, and WHITTINGTON, Dorothy. (1995). *The cost of caring : final report of a longitudinal study of the circumstances of carers.* Compiled for the Equal Opportunities Commission for Northern Ireland by the Centre for Health and Social Research at the University of Ulster. p.70
12. GLENDINNING, Caroline. (1992). *The costs of informal care : looking inside the household.* London: HMSO. (Social Policy Research Unit publication). p.103
13. PARKER, Gillian. (1990). *With due care and attention.* London: Family Policy Studies Centre. p.93

14. HOLZHAUSEN, Emily, and PEARLMAN, Vicky. (2000). *Caring on the breadline : the financial implications of caring.* London: National Carers' Association. p.19

15. ATKIN, Karl, and ROLLINGS, Janet. (1996). Looking after their own? : family care-giving among Asian and Afro-Caribbean communities, *Race and community care.* Edited by W.I.U Ahmad and Karl Atkin. Buckingham: Open University Press. p.80

16. HUNT, Audrey. (1978). *The elderly at home.* London: HMSO. pp.68-86

17. EVASON, Eileen, and WHITTINGTON, Dorothy. (1995). *The cost of caring.* p.27

18. PARKER, Gillian. (1990). *With due care and attention.* p.43

19. ATKIN, Karl, and ROLLINGS, Janet. (1996). Looking after their own? p.80

20. BRIGGS, Anna, and OLIVER, Judith. (1985). *Caring.* London: Routledge & Kegan Paul. p.xviii

21. LAWSON, Dot, and PARKER, Gillian. (1994). *Different types of care : different kinds of carers.* London: HMSO. p.88

22. ATKIN, Karl, and TWIGG, Julia. (1994). *Carers perceived.* p.9

23. EVASON, Eileen, and WHITTINGTON, Dorothy. (1995). *The cost of caring.* p.32

24. FISHER, Mike. (1994). Man made care : community care and older carers, *British Journal of Social Work* (Oxford: Clarendon), No.24. p.669

25. WENGER, Clare. (1992). *Help in old age : facing up to change : a longitudinal network study.* Liverpool: Liverpool University Press. p.204

26. HENWOOD, Melanie. (1998). *Ignored and invisible? : carers' experience of the National Health Service.* London: Carers' National Association. p.47

27. WENGER, Clare. (1992). *Help in old age.* p.205

28. FISHER, Mike. (1994). Man made care. pp.660-661

29. *ibid.*

30. ATKIN, Karl, and TWIGG, Julia. (1994). *Carers perceived.* p.9

31. WENGER, Clare. (1992). *Help in old age.* p.27

32. BULMER, Martin. (1986). *Neighbours : the work of Philip Abrams.* Cambridge: Cambridge University Press. p.30

33. SOCIAL Policy & Administration. (1993). Age speaks for itself in Europe, Special edition: *Social Policy & Administration* (Oxford: Blackwell), Vol.27, no.3. p.197

34. WENGER, Clare. (1992). *Help in old age.* p.28

35. FISHER, Mike. (1994). Man made care. p.667

36. AHMAD, Waqar I.U. (1996). Family obligations and social change among Asian communities, *Race and community care.* Edited by Waqar I.U. Ahmad and Karl Atkin. Buckingham: Open University Press. p.57

37. HICKS, Cherrill. (1988). *Who cares? : looking after people at home.* London: Virago. Quoted in: *Community care : a reader.* Edited by J. Bornat ... [et al]. Basingstoke: Macmillan. pp.185-189

38. CECIL, Rosanne, OFFER, John, and ST. LEGER, Fred. (1987). *Informal welfare : a sociological study of care in Northern Ireland.* Aldershot: Gower. pp.21, 23

39. JANOWITZ, M. (1952). *The community press in an urban setting.* Glencoe, Ill: Free Press.

40. HUNTER, A.H, and SUTTLES, G.D. (1972). The expanding community of limited liability, *The social construction of communities.* Edited by G.D. Suttles. Chicago, Ill: University of Chicago Press. pp.47-48

41. BULMER, Martin. (1987). *The social basis of community care.* London: Unwin Hyman. p.87

7

IS THE IDEA OF COMMUNITY REALISTIC OR POSSIBLE IN MODERN ECONOMIC AND SOCIAL CONDITIONS?

Is the idea of community realistic today? Pessimistic perspectives – Is there a simple contrast between modern society and older societies? – Alternative perspectives: was society in medieval Europe completely different from modern society? – Alternative perspectives: is the process of change in modern society simple and strtaightforward? – Conclusion: the limits of community in modern society

> The future is never entirely determined by the past,
> nor is it ever entirely detached
>
> Arthur Stanley Eddington, The Decline of Determinism, *New Pathways in Science*

Is the idea of community realistic today? Pessimistic perspectives

In 1974 Raymond Plant asked if community work might not be engaged in an impossible enterprise, of seeking to foster community in modern urban industrial society.[1]

Such doubts about the idea of community in 'modern society' continue. The belief is expressed that people's lives are determined increasingly by forces elsewhere and that economic changes on a global scale and the social and cultural consequences of those changes undermine local responses to them. For example, the United Nations Research Institute for Social Development (1995) considered that migration, urbanisation and mass media exposure to global consumer culture had undermined local capacity to respond cohesively to changing circumstances.

The economic forces for change which the Institute identified were an accelerated integration of the world economy and the mobility of global capital. The mobility of capital had been facilitated by computerised dealing systems which dispatched "huge sums of money" across national boundaries.[2] Nigel Harris and Ida Fabricius (1996) observed how the development and applications of new technologies – in particular, jumbo jets, sea freight containers and the international telephone network – had transformed communications and costs throughout the world.[3]

Even an area or local economy which is considered to be successful may be characterised by fragmentation. Martin Boddy, Christine Lambert and Dawn Snare (1997) observed the emergence of new service-based activities and financial services and office centres in the town of Swindon in Southern England between 1970 and 1990, following the decline of the rail engineering industry for which Swindon had been known. They referred to the new enterprises as "a coincidence of enterprises" which happened to share preferences for Swindon's advantages as a location. They viewed Swindon as a satellite to London and to global economic structures. [4]

In modern society social ties and loyalties in general and local ties and loyalties in particular are undermined, it is believed, by economic change. In its survey of the social effects of globalisation, the U.N. Research Institute for Social Development considered that unemployment, crime and drugs had weakened society even in the richer countries.[5] Martin Bulmer (1987), in his synthesis of the work of Philip Abrams on neighbours, neighbouring and neighbourhoods emphasised Philip Abrams' conclusion that it was necessary to recognise the primacy of self interest as a factor in social relationships. Philip Abrams believed that it was necessary to base social care planning on people's expectation of reciprocal care, *i.e.* care for themselves when in need in return for care which they might give to others. He accepted the argument that modern society was pushing individuals towards those commitments which were deemed to be more profitable.[6] In their study of New York, John H. Mollenkopf and Manuel Castells (1991) contrasted what they saw as the increasingly local concerns of communities with the increasingly global perspective of New York's elite.[7]

Pessimism about the social consequences of 'modern society' is not new. Robert Nisbet (1970) identified the 'rediscovery of community' as the most important development in 19th century social thought.[8] He saw this rediscovery of community as a reaction against the individualism of the previous age and the perceived social consequences of the industrial revolution and urbanisation. A particular theme of much of this new interest in community was the supposed contrast between the state of social existence in modern society and in older societies, especially in medieval Europe. As scholars of this new interest in community and of the supposed communal character of medieval European society, Robert Nisbet pointed to Auguste Comte, Otto von Gierke and Ferdinand Tönnies.

It was Ferdinand Tönnies who coined the terms '*gemeinschaft*' and '*gesellschaft*', loosely translated as 'community' and 'association', to describe two contrasting types and qualities of social relationship. He identified *gemeinschaft* more with older, more traditional society and *gesellschaft* more with modern society and urban life. '*Gemeinschaft'* type relationships came to us from nature and the relationships which came to us from nature were in essence mutual.[9] The pillars of '*gemeinschaft*' were "blood, place (or land) and mind or kinship, neighbourhood and friendship ..."[10] By contrast, '*gesellschaft*' type relationships represented rational will,[11] and were based on comparisons of possible and future services.[12] '*Gesellschaft*' society was conceived as "mere coexistence of people independent of each other."[13] '*Gesellschaft*' was associated especially with modern industrial and commercial society and with cities. Tönnies considered that city life, despite its benefits, undermined the home, family life and personal relationships: "only in the city [compared to villages and towns] does the household become sterile, narrow and empty ... a mere living place..."[14] Tönnies viewed family life as the basis of life in the '*gemeinschaft'* : "Family life ... subsists in village and town life ... the village community and the town themselves can be considered as large families ..." [15] However, family life was decaying in the city and especially in the metropolis.[16]

Ferdinand Tönnies' assessment of the impact of the city on social ties and relationships was echoed by Louis Wirth in his 1938 essay 'Urbanism as a Way of Life'. He argued that "The city is characterised by secondary rather than primary contacts.. The contacts of the city may include face-to-face contacts, but they are nevertheless impersonal, superficial, transitory and segmental ..." [17]

Is there a simple contrast between modern society and older societies?

There is one consistent characteristic of such perspectives as are outlined above. They represent an interpretation of the process of historical or social change as a simple, continuous progression, which then can be interpreted either as decline or as development. In the pessimistic perspective outlined above, it is supposed that people's lives have been shaped increasingly by decisions taken elsewhere rather than locally, and by forces which are increasingly global in scale rather than local or national as in the past.

There has been, it is supposed, a fundamental shift in the nature and quality of personal and social relationships in modern society compared to older, more traditional societies. Local ties and associations, frequent face-to-face contacts and the recognition of mutual obligations have given way to more detached, more calculated and more individualistic relations with other people.

Family life which is the basis for social institutions in older, more traditional societies and kin ties which were recognised generally in the older societies have decayed, it is supposed, in modern society, especially in large cities. And such changes are evident especially in the comparison between medieval and modern society in Europe.

But simple pessimism as much as simple optimism distorts the reality of relations between people and between groups of people, and of changes in those relations over time. This distortion is especially likely to occur when a group of people is conceived of as a whole – even as a unit – because they have something in common. When a group of people is conceived of as a whole, as a unit, then past and present are more likely to be interpreted in the singular. What has happened to them in the past, what is happening to them now in the present is determined by the past and present of the group; and within this framework of interpretation, it is easier to see people's past and present in terms of a simple (in the sense that it is singular) progression from one state of affairs to another state of affairs.

Arthur James Balfour (1892) expressed an intense, cohesive, conservative, Victorian vision of community in which people were bound unconsciously but indissolubly by "a thousand ties ... woven out of common sentiments, common tasks, common beliefs ... common prejudices." Nevertheless, he warned of the limits of the power of community. "We habitually talk as if a self governing or free community was one which managed its own affairs ... It manages but a narrow fringe of its affairs ..." [18]

Arthur James Balfour's comments touched on the belief that there had been a time and a society in which people could and did live their lives mainly in relation to one place, within close networks of family and kin ties, and were engaged in a high level of cooperative activity with neighbours. Such a society would be characterised by a low level of social mobility. But when has such a society existed? Such a society, such a state of relations may not have existed among even primitive, pre-literate societies. Philippe De Scola (1992) acknowledged that there was a strong tradition among ethnographers* to describe small, pre-literate groups living within clearly defined territories as if each group was a complete, self-contained whole with a distinct, self-contained culture and set of rules: a complete society. However, he claimed that many ethnographers admitted that people living within the groups the ethnographers studied did not see their groups in this way.[19]

* ETHNOGRAPHY: The direct observation of customs and behaviour in a particular society

The practice of trade can throw some light on this matter. Trade is interesting for what it says about a person's life within and beyond his/her group. The most elementary trading transaction requires a person to go out beyond the boundaries of his/her group. It requires not only the interaction between persons in which the terms of trade are negotiated and goods exchanged, but also earlier encounters and interactions in which the possibilities for trade are identified. And those encounters and interactions require movement out from and movement between groups.

The practice and the history of trade can support Matt Ridley's argument that human groups were not and never had been closed.[20] Brian Fagan (1997) reported evidence from archaeological excavations which indicated that exchange and trade were part of human life and human societies from very ancient times. For example, shells from the Black Sea had been found in late Iron Age encampments at least eighteen thousand years old, deep inside what is now the Ukraine. And finds in North America indicate that the Palaeo-Indians of the Great Plains exchanged fine-grained, tool-making stone over long distances as early as 9,000 B.C.[21]

Alternative perspectives: was society in Mediaeval Europe completely different from modern society?

There has been a tradition which has viewed Europe in the Middle Ages as a time and a society in which people lived their lives mainly in relation to one place, within close networks of family and kin ties, and in which social relationships were based largely on custom and tradition. For example, Robert Nisbet (1970 – see above) observed a renewal of interest in nineteenth century thinking in the idea of community, and a related renewal of interest in the supposed communal past of medieval Europe. More recently, Anthony Giddens in the original edition of his standard *Sociology* (1989) claimed that the household and the local community were the chief focus for the production of goods and services in medieval times.[22] *

Jeannine Quillet (1988) did describe the three centuries from 1150 A.D. as a period which saw a rapid expansion in the forms of social existence in Europe such as associations, leagues, colleges and fraternities.[23] Susan Reynolds (1984) referred to "the medieval drive to association." [24] But the social dynamism which saw this expansion in collective forms of association was reflected also in population growth and movement, in the decline of economic relationships based on custom, in the development of trade and capitalist enterprise, in the growth of towns and cities. Robert Bartlett (1993) pointed out that (allowing for the difficulty of arriving at population figures for the period) the two centuries from 1100 to 1300 A.D. were a time of growth in the population of Europe; and that by 1300 A.D. whole zones of Europe, especially in Eastern Europe, had experienced planned settlement on a large scale.[25] Janet Coleman (1988) observed that by 1300 A.D. the monetary evaluation of land had supplanted rights to land based on customary relationships.[26] Antony Black (1988) noted that in this period the development of commerce and credit and the formation of urban communes both coincided with increasing social and geographical mobility.[27]

The expansion in the use and in the production of money, and the growth and expansion of financial institutions on an international scale, was a characteristic of the later Middle Ages in Europe. Janet Coleman (1988) noted an increasing use of money, a massive increase in the minting of new money, and the development of an elaborate structure of financial credit. This both reflected and facilitated the commercial revolution of the period which produced a market economy centred on towns.[28] John Dunning (1993) estimated that by 1400 A.D. there were as many as one hundred and fifty Italian banking companies operating multi-nationally.[29]

Population movement and resettlement and the growth of towns in the Middle Ages may have reflected both necessities

---

* This claim is absent in later editions of Anthony Giddens' book

forced onto people and choices made by them. Susan Reynolds (1984) observed that as towns grew, guilds and fraternities multiplied in proportion to the separate groups and interests which appeared in the towns.[30] The guilds and fraternities multiplied, she believed, partly because they offered people the warmth and social existence they needed after being uprooted from their homes and families.[31] But the towns offered people new personal and cultural as well as economic opportunities: they saw more of life.[32]

The picture which Susan Reynolds painted of Europe in the Middle Ages can seem modern in relation to the process of urbanisation and to the migration of people to towns and cities and the means by which they sought to adapt to life in towns and cities. Or perhaps it is not 'modern' or 'medieval', but represents a recurring theme and pattern in human societies about how people move and change, and the forms of association in which they become involved as part of the process of adaptation to change.

Europe in the Middle Ages was a society which was complex (which society is not?) and was not static: people changed and moved. It was a society which saw a rapid expansion in the forms of social existence. People today may be surprised by the degree of individual and personal choice and of flexibility with which, often, people led their lives. Even in the supposedly more conservative countryside Susan Reynolds (1984) observed that although the country people of Western Europe were highly collective in their habits and attitudes, they were very flexible about the social units within which they acted.[33]

This individual and personal choice and flexibility of practice was evident in medieval attitudes to family and marriage. Anthony Giddens (1989) has admitted that many sociologists used to suppose that the predominant form of the family in medieval Europe was the extended family, but that more recent research had disproved this.[34] The *Encyclopaedia Britannica* (1992) acknowledged that the change towards nuclear family structure had taken place in Northern Europe long before the fourteenth century.[35] Michael M. Sheehan

(1996) criticised what he judged to be a simplistic understanding of the transition from the extended family structure to the nuclear family structure. He noted the abandonment of the idea that industrialisation and urbanisation were the reasons for the change, which abandonment he attributed to the rapid increase in the number of historical studies of the family (which included his own).[36]

Marriages took place on a more personal, individual and freely-chosen basis than has been recognised often. From his own and other studies of medieval marriage law, using church court records, Michael Sheehan (1994) argued that by the twelfth century, the matrimonial bond was considered to be created and the marriage judged valid, simply on the basis of consent between the two marriage partners. By and large lordship and lords were ignored, and little attention was paid to the wider family circle.[37]

An individualistic theory of marriage, which saw marriage from the point of view of the couple rather than of the extended family network, was taught and practised by the Church. This individualistic view of marriage was underlined by bars on the later dissolution of marriages. Even, private, clandestine marriages could be and were recognised.[38] Nor was this individualistic practice and validation of marriage confined to some people of wealth and power: towards the end of the fourteenth century it was clear that many marriages were private acts, simply performed, and therefore open to even the poorest citizens.[39]

Alternative perspectives: is the process of change in modern society simple and straightforward?

The society of Europe in the Middle Ages can seem to carry echoes of the modern society of today in terms of trade and banking, and population involvement, and the development of town and city life; with many people, perhaps, suffering the effects of dislocation, but with many people also seeking new opportunities. The Middle Ages in Europe saw more people exercising real individual and personal choice about how to lead their lives than is recognised often today. For example, many people exercised real choice about where and how they sought to make a living. Many people exercised real, personal choice about who they married and how they married, with the wider family or kin network not being important in the decision.

It seems that many of the economic and social trends which we regard as being characteristic of present-day society emerged at a much earlier time. But if the progression from past to present is continuous, then all we may be saying here is that the progression to our 'modern society' took place over a longer period of time than has been supposed before; and that our modern society is characterised still by an increasing integration of the world economy, by the global mobility of capital and by a process of population movement and urbanisation which undermines family and kin ties. This (it may be supposed) is what we have been moving towards steadily over a period of time.

But change is rarely so simple or so uniform; and often what is considered to be modern has happened before. Some of the economic trends described under the heading of 'globalisation' are not new. Gordon L. Clarke and Kevin O'Connor (1997) criticised the view that the global integration of the financial services industry was a new phenomenon, and pointed to studies such as L. Neal's which described the global nature of the industry in the seventeenth, eighteenth and nineteenth centuries.[40] Indeed the perceived integration of the economically advanced world's financial system may have been greater in the recent past than in the present day. Paul Hirst and Grahame Thompson (1996) noted that there had been earlier periods of internationalisation of trade and the monetary system, especially between 1870 and 1914. The international financial markets in the late nineteenth and early twentieth centuries were more fully integrated than they had been before or have been since. The international financial penetration of the United Kingdom economy, for example, was greater between 1900 and 1914 than it was in the late 1980's. Similarly the foreign trade of the U.K between 1900 and 1914 represented a greater percentage of Gross Domestic Product than in the late 1980's.[41]

Are the processes of change today simple and straightforward? Are we seeing a comprehensive integration of the world's economies, and global mobility of capital? There is continuing debate. John Dunning (1997) argued that economic activity by companies and by countries was being organised and integrated increasingly across international borders.[42] However, the *Economist* argued in its 'Survey of Globalisation' (2001) that international economic integration was far from complete, and was likely to remain so. As an example, it referred to investment. International investment, it claimed, was less important than domestic investment in most countries.[43]

The *Economist* blamed governments and politicians for using the supposed demands of globalisation to deny responsibility. It argued that governments had more capacity to act independently than they acknowledged. For example: governments around the world were collecting more taxes from their citizens than they were ten years ago.

Meric S. Gertier (1997) complained of the tendency to confuse finance capital with other forms of capital. Referring to case studies of Canadian firms, and of German firms active in Canada, the USA and elsewhere, Meric Gertier argued that fixed capital, especially advanced machinery, was much more rooted to place. The majority of firms surveyed preferred to obtain advanced machinery from the same country and preferably from the same region. A majority of firms in Ontario, for example, were found to be significantly more likely to experience difficulties in operating advanced machinery from Europe or Japan than from North America. Although the social or cultural context in which machinery was designed might contribute to such operating difficulties, Meric Gertier concluded that it was easier to communicate complex technical information about advanced machinery face-to-face rather than attempt to do so over long distances, even with the aid of modern communications technology.[44]

Alternative perspectives: family and kin ties and social networks in modern society

There may be room to doubt that there is a simple and comprehensive process of globalisation. There may be room also to doubt that there is a simple and comprehensive process of urbanisation which undermines family and kin ties (and encourages more detached, more calculated and more self-interested relations with other people).

Thomas C. Wilson (1993) sought to test four generalisations about the effects of urbanism on kin and kinship bonds: that urbanism retards family completeness; that it promotes kin dispersal; that it engenders disregard of kin; that it alters functions served by kin.[45] The basis of his study was the N.O.R.C. 1986 General Social Survey in the United States. This survey was comprehensive not only in providing data for the whole of the United States, but in taking account of telephone and written communications between people, as well as direct face-to-face contacts. (Thomas Wilson criticised some other studies on the effects of urbanism because they confined themselves to data based on face-to-face contacts).

He found no evidence in this study that urbanism promoted disregard of kin. Nor apparently had urbanism any adverse effects on the functions served by kin. And although urbanism did reduce proximity and face-to-face contact with extended relatives, contact through telephone calls and letters increased.

The survey provided little evidence that urbanism diminished bonds based on kinship, and provided evidence that in general bonds based on kinship were maintained. It also provided evidence that urbanism could enrich the potential for non-kinship bonds.[45]

Yossi Shavit, Claude Fischer and Yael Koresh (1994) noted that it was a common finding of research on disasters and crises that people turned overwhelmingly to kin for support. They reported on their study of how people in Israel used their social networks for support in the face of Scud missile attacks from Iraq during the 1991 Gulf War. The outbreak of war coincided with a pilot for a general survey of Israeli social networks. The war and the missile attacks seemed to offer the researchers a rare opportunity to examine how people used their social networks in the face of a mortal threat. Their study focused on Haifa, a major port and industrial centre, and the third largest city in Israel. (They considered that in general the population of Haifa was "somewhat more affluent and educated" than the population of Israel as a whole). The study indicated that the people interviewed relied on kin more than on 'everyday' networks. The comfort and advice of conversation was provided often by friends; but for more immediate and direct aid people turned overwhelmingly to kin.[46]

Even when there is a perception of breakdown in the relevance of local or national boundaries as a framework for social networks, in the face of population movement on an international scale, there can be also a sense of the enduring elasticity of family, kin and wider social networks as they persist across larger spaces and longer distances. Michael Peter Smith (1995) acknowledged that an increasing number of household, kinship and formerly village-based social networks extended across national boundaries. They had become bi-national or multi-national in terms of the space they occupied.[47]

Conclusion: the limits of community in modern society

The belief that the idea of community is not realistic in modern society, especially when modern society is compared to older, more traditional societies, stems from an exaggeration of the significance of community. Community may be exaggerated as a basis for defining people's social existence in older, supposedly more traditional societies. Consequently there is a corresponding sense of the decline of community in modern society. This sense of decline of community runs parallel to and encourages and is encouraged by an over-simplification of the processes of change in society in the past and in the present time. Over-simplification is evident in the instinct to see historical change as a simple, continuous progression from the past to the present time, to 'modern society'. (And what is modern society or modern times but the particular point of time and space at which someone happens to be speaking or writing?)

Community may be exaggerated also in the degree to which, it is assumed, people's identities and relationships with each other are defined by the boundaries of the group or association – or community – in which they are involved, with which they are identified. But does any person see himself/herself simply as belonging to a particular group or association or community? And are the groups, associations, institutions or networks which may be identified with a particular place likely to take in all or most of the relationships of the people living there?

The idea of community is not validated by exaggerations of the significance of community or of the decline of community in past or present times. Nor is the idea of community invalidated by the incompleteness of groups, associations, institutions or networks in relation to the people who are supposed to be involved in or identified with them. Community can represent one dimension of our social existence, of our relations with other people. What the incompleteness of groups, associations, institutions or networks demonstrate are the limits to the relevance of the idea of community.

REFERENCES

1. PLANT, Raymond. (1974). *Community and ideology : an essay in applied social philosophy*. London: Routledge & Kegan Paul. p.28

2. UNITED NATIONS Research Institute for Social Development. (1995). *States of disarray : social effects of globalisation*. Geneva: UNRISD. pp.17, 26

3. FABRICIUS, Ida, and HARRIS, Nigel. (1996). *Cities and cultural adjustment*. London: UCL Press. pp.20-21

4. BODDY, Martin, LAMBERT, Christine, and SNARE, Dawn. (1997). City for the twenty-first century? : planning and urban change in contemporary Britain, *Contemporary Britain*. Bristol: Policy Press. p.311

5. UNITED NATIONS Research Institute for Social Development. (1995). *States of disarray*. p.28

6. BULMER, Martin. (1986). *The work of Philip Abrams.* Cambridge: Cambridge University Press. p.104

7. CASTELLS, Manuel, and MOLLENKOPF, John H. (1991). Is New York a dual city?, *Dual city : restructuring New York.* New York: Russell Sage Foundation. p.416

8. NISBET, Robert. (1970). *The sociological tradition.* London: Heinemann. p.47

9. TÖNNIES, Ferdinand. (1931). Gemeinschaft und Gesellschaft, *Handworter Buch der Soziologie.* Stuttgart: Ferdinand Enke. p.20. Quoted in: *Community and association (Gemeinschaft und gessellschaft)* / Ferdinand Tönnies. Translated and supplemented by Charles P. Loomis. London: Routledge & Kegan Paul, 1955. p.20

10. TÖNNIES, Ferdinand. (1887-). *Community and association.* Translated by Charles P. Loomis. p.223

11. TÖNNIES, Ferdinand. (1931). Gemeinschaft und Gesellschaft. p.17

12. TÖNNIES, Ferdinand. (1887-). *Community and association.* p.89

13. *ibid.* p.38

14. *ibid.* p.187

15. *ibid.* p.267

16. *ibid.* p.269

17. WIRTH, Louis. (1938). Urbanism as a way of life, *American Journal of Sociology* (Chicago: University of Chicago Press). Vol.44, no.1. pp.12, 20-21

18. BALFOUR, Arthur James. (1893). A fragment on progress, *Essays and addresses.* 2nd ed. Edinburgh: David Douglas. p.274

19. DE SCOLA, Philippe. (1992). Societies of nature and the nature of society, *Conceptualising society.* Edited by Adam Kuper. London: Routledge. p.107

20. RIDLEY, Matt. (1996). *The origins of virtue.* Harmonsdworth: Penguin/Viking. p.200

21. FAGAN, Brian M. (1997). *In the beginning.* 9th ed. New York: Longman. p.358

22. GIDDENS, Anthony. (1989). *Sociology.* Cambridge: Polity. p.390

23. QUILLET, Jeannine. (1988). Community, counsel and representation, *The Cambridge history of medieval political thought.* Edited by J.H. Burns. Cambridge: Cambridge University Press. pp.525, 537

24. REYNOLDS, Susan. (1984). *Kingdoms and communities in Western Europe, 900-1300 A.D.* Oxford: Clarendon. p77

25. BARTLETT, Robert. (1993). *The making of Europe : conquest, colonisation and cultural change.* Harmondsworth: Penguin. p170

26. COLEMAN, Janet. (1988). Property and poverty, *The Cambridge history of medieval political thought.* p.616

27. BLACK, Antony. (1988). The individual and society, *The Cambridge history of medieval political thought.* p.593

28. COLEMAN, Janet. (1988). Property and poverty, *The Cambridge history of medieval political thought.* pp.607-608

29. DUNNING, J.H. (1993). *Multi-national enterprise and the global economy.* Wokingham: Addison Wesley. pp.97-98. Quoted in: *Globalisation in question : the international economy and the possibility of governance.* Cambridge: Polity. p.19

30. REYNOLDS, Susan. (1984). *Kingdoms and communities in Western Europe.* p.217

31. *ibid.* p.73

32. *ibid.* p.217

33. *ibid.* p.139

34. GIDDENS, Anthony. (1989). *Sociology.* p.388

35. THE MEDIEVAL Family, *New Encyclopaedia Britannica.* 15th ed. Chicago: Encyclopedia Britannica Inc. Macropedia. Vol.19. p.61

36. SHEEHAN, Michael M. (1994). *Marriage, family and law in medieval Europe : collected studies.* Edited by James K. Farge. Cardiff: University of Wales Press. pp.87-88

37. *ibid.* pp.91-92

38. *ibid.* pp.39-40

39. *ibid.* p.240

40. CLARK, Gordon L, and O'CONNOR, Kevin. (1997). The informational content of financial products and the spatial structure of the global finance industry, *Spaces of globalisation : re-asserting the power of the local.* Edited by Kevin R. Cox. New York: Guildford. p.90

41. HIRST, Paul, and THOMPSON, Grahame. (1996). *Globalisation in question : the international economy and the politics of governance.* Cambridge: Polity. pp.195, 36, 196

42. DUNNING, John H. (1997). *Alliance, capitalism and global business.* London: Routledge. p.34

43. SURVEY of globalisation, *The Economist* (29th September 2001). pp.16-24

44. GERTIER, Meric S. (1997). Between the global and the local : spatial limits to productive capital, *Spaces of globalisation : reasserting the power of the local.* Edited by Kevin. R. Cox. New York: Guildford. pp.47-53

45. WILSON, Thomas C. (1993). Urbanism and kinship bonds, *Social Forces* (Chapel Hill, NC: University of North Carolina Press). Vol.71, no.3. pp.703-712

46. SHAVIT, Yossi, FISCHER, Claude S, and KORESH, Yael. (1994). Kin and non-kin under collective threat : Israeli networks during the Gulf War, *Social Forces.* Vol.72, no.4. pp.1197-1215

47. SMITH, Michael Peter. (1995). The disappearance of world cities and the globalisation of local politics, *World cities in a world system.* Edited by Paul L. Knox and Peter J. Taylor. Cambridge: Cambridge University Press. pp.250, 255

8

THE IDEA OF COMMUNITY AND THE CONFLICT OF VALUES

The idea of community as a value – Conflicts of values. – Are conflicts of values inevitable? – Community as a value versus other values

> There always exist irresolvable clashes of values; there are many social problems which are insoluble because moral principles may conflict ... there can be no human society without conflict : such a society would be a society, not of friends, but of ants.
>
> Karl Popper, *Unended Quest*

The idea of community as a value

Often the discussion of community expresses what I would call a unitary idea of community : a sense of wholeness in thinking about community and society. There is an assumption that if people have common characteristics – if, for example, they are resident in the same place or if they come from the same ethnic or religious or cultural background – then they represent parts of a whole. References to local community may express an assumption that there exist common relationships, associations and institutions between people who are resident within the same area.

Often in the discussion of community and communities there is a further assumption, of a consensus about goals and values between the people who are included within the bounds of a community. This assumption may be an element in arguments that communities – and not simply people – should be helped to influence or participate in or should be consulted about decisions which affect them. It may be an element in arguments that communities can help to provide services for people who need support because of illness or disability; or that people who are leaving institutions should be helped to re-integrate with the community.

Raymond Williams (1983) noted that community was unlike all other terms of social organisation in that it seemed never to be used unfavourably.[1] It was a 'good thing'. As well as 'community' being used as a term of social organisation, the idea of community itself can be seen as a value or as a set of values: that is part of its enduring appeal. Anthony Cohen (1985) identified community as a system of values and moral codes which provided its members with a sense of identity.[2] Robert Nisbet (1970) enthused that community was "founded on man conceived in his wholeness" and that community was "a fusion of feeling and thought, of tradition and commitment, of membership and volition." [3]

Conflicts of values

However, it can be argued that any society can, and most societies do, give rise to conflicts of values. A conflict of values may arise most directly in the inclusion of some people within a group or form of association and the exclusion others. Graham Crow and Graham Allan (1994) argued that communities gained much of their coherence by being exclusive.[4]

People's own personal values may change over time, and so come into conflict with the values of other people in their group or society. Mary Midgley (1994) pointed to people who had been brought up in slave-owning communities who had in many cases gradually come to see slavery as being wrong and had contributed to its eventual abolition – "That was possible because they had within them other attitudes, other ideals, other perceptions with which slave owning conflicted." [5]

However, it is not necessary to have a conflict of personal moral values for there to be a conflict between the different judgements which people of a particular group or society may have as to which course they should take, or which social policies they should pursue and how they should be managed. Roland Warren (1973) acknowledged that values which might be considered to be the basis for a good community might not support each other. A gain for one value might undermine another.[6] Robin Hambleton (1994), in his survey of urban government in Britain and the USA, foresaw the possibility of a conflict between on the one hand a radical approach to strengthening the accountability of a local authority to "the local neighbourhood" for the provision of services to it, and on the other hand the pursuit of local authority-wide policies with a common objective, *e.g.* promoting opportunities for neglected groups to participate more in society.[7] Two values are expressed in these two policies – on the one hand to give people more influence in the decisions which affect their lives, and on the other hand, to change the circumstances of particular groups of people who are considered to be disadvantaged in society. The possibility of conflict exists because the outcome of one policy may be to strengthen the position of people who are critical of or are opposed to the outcome of the other policy. The local neighbourhood to which the authority seeks to be more accountable may oppose some of the services for disadvantaged groups which the authority seeks to provide throughout its area.

Such conflicts are an inevitable part of the political process in any society and there are no institutional or political forms which can guarantee that such actual or potential conflicts are avoided. The political process, at whatever level, is partly about how such actual or potential conflicts are worked through.

Are conflicts of values inevitable?

Isaiah Berlin (1969) argued that "... not all good things are compatible, still less all the ideals of mankind ..."[8]

Isaiah Berlin considered that Niccolo Machiavelli, the Renaissance political consultant, philosopher and administrator (who has been immortalised in the term 'machiavellian'), introduced a fundamental breach with the previous sense of wholeness in thinking about community and society. He acknowledged that there was something peculiarly disturbing about what Machiavelli said or implied: something that had caused profound and lasting uneasiness.[9] It was not simply

Machiavelli's cynicism and moral pessimism, nor his advocacy of ruthless methods. His cynicism and moral pessimism were not unique, and his advocacy of ruthless methods was not gratuitous. Isaiah Berlin asserted that Machiavelli's cardinal achievement was "his uncovering of an insoluble dilemma, the planting of a permanent question mark in the path to posterity ..." His achievement stemmed from "his *de facto* recognition that ends equally ultimate, equally sacred, may contradict each other; that entire systems of values may come into collision with each other ... and as part of the normal human situation." [10]

Machiavelli, in Isaiah Berlin's view, undermined a major assumption of western thought, that somewhere "... there is to be found the final solution to the question of how men should live." [11] Machiavelli implicitly recognised that there was a pluralism of values between which conscious choices had to be made. He recognised diversity and conflict as inevitable aspects of human relations and society.[12]

Community as a value *versus* other values

If the possibility exists of conflict between values which different people hold sincerely then it must be admitted that the idea of community as a whole may come into conflict with other values. And for some people in some situations, community may not be the greatest value.

Some people may not wish to belong to communities, and may wish to escape from community. For them personal mobility and autonomy may be greater values (see Chapter 8). And community may come to represent for some people values which other people would find objectionable. Jocelyn Cornwell (1984) referred to the 'dark side of community' in her observations on community in East London. There was belonging, but also not belonging. There was inclusion, but also exclusion. There was a dislike of what was different and people who were different.[13]

In Northern Ireland, the Community Development Review Group in 1991 put forward recommendations as to how government and public bodies in Northern Ireland could support a process of community development.[14] The Group asserted that community development was a process which should be governed by principles and values that emphasise equity and an active opposition to prejudice and sectarianism. It emphasised also the importance of statutory agencies being responsive to the views of local communities. But what if people from some local communities express views which you believe to represent prejudice and sectarianism? You can either accept the views of those people, or oppose their views; or seek to persuade them to think differently (and what do you do if you do not succeed in persuading them?)

David Cesarani (1993), in an assessment of the British National Party's victory in a 1993 bye-election for Tower Hamlets Council in London, asserted that the racism which he considered the BNP's victory to express was a "... belligerent and deeply objectionable defence of community." He went on to ask: "How can we create vibrant neighbourhoods that are not also ethnically defensive?" [15]

But neighbourhoods and communities, vibrant or otherwise, cannot be *created.* The desire to 'create' communities of a particular character represents a failure to come to terms with this particular limit to the significance of community when considered as a value: that in some situations perhaps community should be considered as a lesser value or perhaps should be rejected as a negative value.

REFERENCES

1. WILLIAMS, Raymond. (1983). *Keywords.* London: Fontana Paperbacks. p.76

2. COHEN, Anthony. (1989). *The symbolic construction of community.* London: Routledge.

3. NISBET, Robert. (1970). *The sociological tradition.* London: Heinemann. pp.47-48

4. ALLAN, Graham, and CROW, Graham. (1994). *Community life : an introduction to local social relations.* Hemel Hempstead: Harvester Wheatsheaf. p.10

5. MIDGLEY, Mary. (1994). *The ethical primate.* London: Routledge. pp.152-153
6. WARREN, Roland L. (1973). The good community : what could it be?, *Perspectives on the American community.* Chicago: Rand McNally College Publishing. p.475
7. HAMBLETON, Robin. (1994). New directions for urban government in Britain and America, *Policy and change.* Edited by Randal Smith and Jane Raistrick. Bristol: SAUS Publications. p.137
8. BERLIN, Isaiah. (1969). Two concepts of liberty, *Liberty.* Edited by Henry Hardy. Oxford: OUP, 2002. p.213 [1]
9. BERLIN, Isaiah. (1979). The originality of Machiavelli, *Against the current.* Oxford: OUP, 1981. p.26 [2]
10. *ibid.* pp.74-75
11. *ibid.* p.76
12. *ibid.* p.75
13. CORNWELL, Jocelyn. (1984). *Hard-earned lives : accounts of health and illness in East London.* London: Tavistock. p.55
14. COMMUNITY DEVELOPMENT Review Group. (1991). Summary of recommendations, *Community development in Northern Ireland : perspectives for the future.* [Belfast]
15. CESARANI, David. (1993). Between a rock and a hard place, *The Guardian* (21 September 1993). p.20

---

[1] 'Two concepts of liberty' first published in: *Four essays on liberty* / Isaiah Berlin. London: OUP, 1969

[2] Original publication: *Against the current : essays in the history of ideas* / Isaiah Berlin. Edited by Henry Hardy.. London: Hogarth, 1979

9

THE MULTIPLICITY OF COMMUNITIES

To talk about a 'community' and to refer to someone as belonging to a community suggests a particular group of people who are distinct from other people who do not belong to that group, although they may belong to other groups. It is a way of talking about community which is characterised by a sense of social limits: some people belong and other people, outside of the boundaries which define the group, do not. For example, if you live in a place which is identified with or as a particular community (a housing estate, or a neighbourhood, or a village or whatever) or if you belong to an ethnic or cultural or religious group – then you are considered to be part of the community which is identified with that place or group: you belong.

The belief that people belong to particular communities may encourage assumptions about each person's social existence. For example, there is the assumption that a person can be identified with a particular community whatever the actual state of his/her relationships (see Introduction and Chapter 5). Or there is the assumption expressed in what I would describe as a sense of unitary community: that if different people share characteristics – if they are resident in the same place, or if they come from the same cultural or religious or ethnic backgrounds, or if they share personal problems or interests – then they represent parts of a whole.

Raymond Plant in *Community and Ideology* (1974) recognised a tension between the freedom of the individual and the cooperation and fraternity associated with community, and asked: how could the two ideas be held together? He was attracted to the idea of membership. Only the idea of membership, he believed, filled both a commitment to the individual and a commitment to community.[1]

But is it realistic to interpret our social existence in this way? 'Membership' is both a simple and an inclusive way of interpreting our social relationships (*i.e.* our relationships with each other beyond the personal and the intimate). It is simple in that it promotes an interpretation of our social relationships essentially in terms of the groups or forms of association with which we are involved or to which we are attached. It is inclusive in that it promotes an either/or interpretation of involvement with or attachment to particular groups or associations. Either a person is a part of a particular group or association – or community – or he/she is not.

The idea of membership encourages an interpretation of community in terms of different social units, with an individual person belonging to, being a member of a particular community while another person may belong to, be a member of a different community.

But I would argue that the reality of our social existence, and the reality of who we are, is that most of us are involved in a multiplicity of common interests and interactions and a multiplicity of forms of association. The great Ulster poet John Hewitt (1974), speaking from within a society in conflict in Northern Ireland – where issues of identity and loyalty have been at the heart of the conflict – expressed a strong sense of personal identity by emphasising the *variety* of places with which he identified. These various groups and places were not alternatives to each other: rather they related to each other:

> *I'm an Ulsterman of planter stock. I was born in the island of Ireland, so secondarily I'm an Irishman. I was born in the British archipelago and English is my native tongue, so I am British. The British archipelago consists of offshore islands to the continent of Europe, so I am European.* [2]

These were what John Hewitt described as his 'hierarchy of values'. He insisted that omitting even one step falsified the situation.

The logic of such an outlook is that social existence is inescapably plural. A person's involvement in or attachment to one particular group is partial and relative: it is part of a more general picture. A person's involvement in or attachment to one particular group cannot be isolated from involvement in or attachment to another. Each group which a person is involved in or attached to is an element in that person's social existence.

Another person from the same part of the world or from the same society might see himself/herself rather differently; and he/she might arrange his/her personal hierarchy of values and the balance of his/her attachments and associations rather differently. But he/she could still share attachments and associations with the first person.

REFERENCES

1. PLANT, Raymond. (1974). *Community and ideology*. London: Routledge & Kegan Paul. p.50
2. HEWITT, John. (1974). In: *The Irish Times* (4th July 1974). Quoted in: *The selected John Hewitt*. Edited by Alan Warner. Belfast: Blackstaff, 1981. p.6

10

DOES EVERYBODY WANT TO BELONG TO A COMMUNITY?

They have cradled you in custom,
They have primed you with their preaching
They have put you in a showcase:
You're a credit to their teaching –
But can't you hear the wild? – it's calling you.
Let us probe the silent places,
Let us seek what luck betides us;
Let us journey to a lonely land I know.
There's a whisper on the night-wind,
There's a star gleam to guide us.
And the wild is calling, calling ... let us go.
Robert W. Service, *The Call of the Wild*

Colin Bell and Howard Newby (1971) declared that everyone – even sociologists – wanted to belong to a community.[1] Robert Nozick (1974) assumed that each of us lives in particular communities.[2]

Are such claims true of everyone or at all times? Sometimes the simple personal, possibly instinctive choices which people make in their lives qualify or even contradict such claims. For example, people may live in the same place and face the same situation but make different personal choices in reacting to that situation. Michael Langstaff and Michael Gibson, in their study of urban renewal (1982), drew on surveys of the housing redevelopment process in Leeds and Liverpool. They criticised what they referred to as the myth of people facing redevelopment who reacted as one either to oppose housing clearance or to welcome it. Attitudes were formed on a more individual basis. People weighed up the net gains and losses to each one of them of moving as compared to staying.[3] Raymond Pahl (1984) reported on the Isle of Sheppey which he described as a small, relatively self-contained island community in the

Thames estuary, with a long tradition of employment in the dockyards and other traditional industries. Raymond Pahl found that the views and aspirations of the residents had diverged from each other as their fortunes diverged, especially as traditional industries declined. People thought more in terms of individual goals than of collective goals, and more of private plans than of collective action.[4]

Sometimes people may interpret group situations in terms of very personal or individual satisfactions. Alison Petch (1994) reported on research during 1988-89 into eleven supported accommodation projects across Scotland for people suffering from mental health problems. The projects aimed to help people move out of hospitals or institutional care into smaller scale 'houses' with supporting staff and services. The research into the projects was based in two hundred and fifty-five detailed interviews with one hundred and forty-five different people. It emerged that prior to the move into supported accommodation, only a minority of those interviewed were looking forward to it; but that after the move, by the time of the first interviews, three quarters of those interviewed preferred living in the houses to where they had been living before. For many, what was most important about the houses was that they provided a source of security and privacy.[5]

People may choose to leave the group or association – or place – in which they have been involved, although it has helped to nurture them, because for them it is time to move on. Marion Malcolm (1992) described such a situation with the Ark Housing Project in Musselburgh in East Scotland. Ark Housing was a voluntary organisation which aimed to provide housing for people with learning difficulties. A local scheme consisted of a house with an average of ten residents, which was considered to be the best number for the houses to be financially and socially viable. A local scheme was promoted only if the local community considered that there was a need for it. The aim of Ark Housing, and of each local scheme, was to help people to be as independent as possible. The local house was intended to provide each resident with a home for life unless and until the resident was ready to leave, and over the period of the scheme's life, half of the residents moved on.[6]

The group may sustain and give strength, but at certain times it is not for everyone. Lami Mulvey and Vicky Hobson (1992) described the Out of House Project in the Craigentinney area of Edinburgh. It was based on a course which aimed to provide educational opportunities for women who were isolated and had little successful experience in work or education. The course was one of a number of projects sponsored by the Craigentinny Health Project which was established in 1987 with support from a number of public bodies and funding from the Lothian Health Board. The primary purpose of the Criaigentinny Health Project was to address issues of health and well-being by providing a network of resources which could be locally based and easily accessible. It was to be based in the community and it was intended to respond to the community's own definition of its needs.

The Out-of-House course itself was based on a range of arts-linked activities and on the practice of communications skills for four hours, one day per week. A crèche and crèche worker were provided to help women with small children to attend. Places on the course were offered to twelve carefully chosen women aged between twenty-three years and sixty-one years. Each of them were interviewed at least twice before the first session. All twelve women attended the first session; but by the fourth week, three different women had withdrawn because of various problems. One of the three women who withdrew said that she found that the group was too large to talk about her problems.[7]

Rejection of group or association may be more far reaching. People may make individual choices that go beyond or outside of the bounds of community. Such individual choices are seen often in a negative sense: as representing an absence or a breakdown of community. But for the people concerned, such individual choices may express a positive sense of difference and a necessary assertion of self. In *Escape Attempts : the Theory and Practice of Resistance to Everyday Life*, Stanley Cohen and Laurie Taylor declared their subject matter to be self *in spite* of the structural order of society. The subjects whom they studied ranged from prisoners affirming their identities within and despite the prison system, to explorers testing their identities in wildernesses.[8]

In expressing difference or asserting self; in breaking away; in going somewhere, in terms of physical space or a state of mind, *alone* – a person may be expressing needs to which the idea of community is not relevant. To accept the reality of these needs and of various 'escape attempts', as Stanley Cohen and Laurie Taylor described them, is not to deny the validity of the idea of community, but to recognise that the idea of community goes only so far. This limit to the relevance of the idea of community is understood more easily if we view community as a dimension of a person's existence instead of viewing it in terms of social units to which a person belongs, of which he/she is a member.

REFERENCES

1. BELL, Colin, and NEWBY, Howard. (1971). *Community studies.* London: Allen & Unwin. p.21
2. NOZICK, Robert. 1974). *Anarchy, state and utopia.* Oxford: Blackwell. p.332
3. GIBSON, Michael, and LANGSTAFF, Michael. (1982). *An introduction to urban renewal.* London: Hutchinson. pp.48-49
4. PAHL, Raymond E. (1984). *Divisions of labour.* Oxford: Blackwell. Quoted in: *Community life : an introduction to local social relations*, by Graham Allan and Graham Crow. Hemel Hempstead: Harvester Wheatsheaf, 1994. pp.55-57
5. PETCH, Alison. (1994). The best move I've made : the role of housing for those with mental health problems, *Caring for people in the community : the new welfare.* Edited by Michael Titterton. London: Jessica Kingsley. pp.81-82
6. MALCOLM, Marion. (1992). Ark Housing in Musselburgh, *Experiences of community care : case studies of UK practice.* Edited by Bruce Lynch and Richard Perry. Harlow: Longman. pp.89-92
7. HOBSON, Vicki, and MULVEY, Lami. (1992). Craigentinny Health Project, *Experiences of community care.* pp.64-75
8. COHEN, Stanley, and TAYLOR, Laurie. (1978). *Escape attempts : the theory and practice of resistance to everyday life.* Harmondsworth: Pelican. pp.120-123, 210

11

COMMUNITY, BELONGING AND SELF

Attachment, association and personal identity – Who decides who a person is? – Being part of a community – Is there an individual self? – The social construction of self: at a simple level – The social construction of self: as a more complex process – The social construction of self: what it does not explain – The self and others: what is distinctive? – The self: do we start with nothing? Is what we become or what we are pre-determined? – The self: unique awareness and unique existence.

To what degree is it realistic to talk of someone as belonging to a community? To say that someone belongs to a particular community is to make a statement about who that person is: a statement about their identity and self. But who decides who that person is and where and with whom he/she belongs? Who is entitled to define that person's identity and self?

These questions touch on the fundamental issue of the relationship of the individual person to society and to association with other people. So to consider how far community goes and what the limits of community may be, it is necessary to examine these issues of belonging, identity and self and who can decide them.

Attachment, association and personal identity

If each person's identity and self – who each of us are and how we see ourselves – is decided by influences outside of ourselves, whether in terms of upbringing, or the personal and social relationships into which we enter, or the cultural and historic traditions we inherit: then each person is to be defined essentially in terms of attachments to and associations with other people, past and present. So to talk of someone as being part of, as belonging to a community is an aspect of defining that person in terms of his/her attachments and associations, past and present.

But if each person's identity and self is determined to some degree at least by that person, by the choices which he or she makes and by what is unique to him or her from the beginning, then that limits the degree to which we can interpret that person in terms of his or her attachments to and associations with other people. Those attachments and associations, although important, will not be all-important in determining that person's identity and self.

Who decides who a person is?

Anthony Cohen (1994) posed the question: who has the right to determine who a person is: the person in question or those with whom that person interacts? I would ask a further question: can you be part of a community and not be aware of it? For if we talk about 'a community' and represent a community as having an objective reality independent of the consciousness of people who are supposed to be part of it, we imply that a person's identity – who he or she is – can be defined by other people.

If we assume that we can know who a person is and where he or she belongs, and we can define that person's identity independently of what that person says, then we open the way to making assumptions about what that person's attitudes, preferences, choices will be independently of what that person says. We open the way to claims being make on that person with regards to his/her supposed obligations to share attitudes or to support or participate in activities or organisations on the grounds of loyalty to the group or to the 'community' to which other people have decided he/she belongs.

We make assumptions about other people – about their identity and where they belong – when we suggest that they are part of a community simply because of the background from which they come. We are suggesting this when, for example, we refer to the community of (A) and have in mind both the people who live within a certain area and also what their connection with each other is. We are suggesting it also when we refer to someone as belonging, for example, to the Chinese community or the Catholic community or the Protestant community or the Black community simply because they are Chinese or Catholic or Protestant or Black, *i.e.* they come from one of those traditions.

And when we suggest that people may be identified as belonging to a particular community because of the background from which they come, we are implying that a community – whatever that is – exists, can have an objective reality independent to some degree at least of the consciousness of people who are supposed to be part of it. (You may not be aware of it, but you can be a part of it nonetheless.)

Of course, the word 'community' might be taken to indicate no more than a group of people who have something in common: they come from the same place or tradition; or they hold membership in the same organisation. So the word community could represent simply a means of categorising people according to perceived common characteristics. It could be seen as another simple word to refer to people in groups.

But the word community is used not only to refer to the grouping together of people who have something in common, to describe what is; but also to express aspirations as to what it is believed ought to be in relationships between people. Most often when the word community is used to expresses values, it is a 'good thing'. Raymond Williams (1983) observed that unlike all other terms of social organisation it seemed never to be used unfavourably.[2] It is not enough to see community as a simple word referring to people in groups. Most people imply more than that when they use it.

Being part of a community

But what if a community is not a matter of objective reality? What if being part of a community is first and foremost a matter of consciousness? In this sense to say that someone else is part of a community is an expression of acceptance and inclusion. In this sense of it the idea of community can be constructed only on a basis of consciousness and choice. Even when people who consider themselves to belong together in a community share some objective characteristics, *e.g.* living within the same locality or coming from the same ethnic or cultural or religious background – it will be their perceptions of themselves and their relationships with each other which will be the essential elements in constructing an idea of community.

So in this sense of the word, belonging to, identifying with a community requires a person to declare: I belong to, I am part of that community. It requires an assertion of self. But such an assertion of self may lead also to a person distancing himself/herself from a particular association or grouping – although he/she shares characteristics and concerns with other people of that association or grouping – and identifying himself/herself more with other associations or groupings.

Is there an individual self?

So an awareness of self can qualify the dimensions of community. But from where does self come? And is there such a thing as an individual self? The individual self has not been accepted always in times past as a significant entity. For example, during the Middle Ages in Europe the use of the word community reflected, according to Jeannine Quillet in *The Cambridge History of Medieval Political Thought* (1988), an organic vision of society. The individual self was not part of this vision.[3]

The individual self is a contested idea today. The self and personal identity often are interpreted as reflecting cultural or social or economic processes. The *International Encyclopaedia of the Social Sciences* (1968) declared that the self was not innate, but was the product of interaction from infancy onwards with the individual's physical and social environment.[4] Peter Berger and Thomas Lucknow (1979) insisted that reality, or our sense of reality, is socially constructed and that identity is formed by social processes.[5] Nancy Rosenberg (1992) described people as 'subjects' who were the creations of a particular social, political and economic world at a certain time.[6]

Even more emphatically, David Sibley (1995) insisted the self is a cultural production which is being perpetually restructured.[7]

So is who we are determined by our interaction with other people? If it is, then our sense of belonging, of where we belong, our consciousness of who we are can be said to be 'socially constructed'. Our identity, our sense of self would have to be seen in terms of where and with whom we belong; in terms of our connection to, our interaction with other people, past and present.

But how much can such a way of interpreting reality – the social construction of self theory – explain? It is necessary to recognise the different levels at which this theory can be implied or be presented, and examine it critically at each level.

The social construction of self : at a simple level

If our connection with other people, our participation in groups and associations, our sense of who we are and where and with whom we belong is socially constructed, it can be presented firstly at a simple level: that is, that our identities, who we are, can be determined directly and simply by our background: either the place and the people with whom each of us live or grow up; or the particular cultural or religious or ethnic groups from which we come. This way of defining our identities is rarely presented as such; it may not be intended; but it is implied often by the way in which personal attachments are discussed. It is implied often by the way in which the idea of local community is expressed: by the way in which supposed local communities are discussed. It is implied by referring to someone as belonging to, for example, the Chinese community, or the Catholic community, or the Protestant community or the Black community simply because he or she is Chinese or Catholic or Protestant or Black, *i.e.* he or she comes from one of those traditions.

The idea that our identities, who we are can be determined directly and simply by our background is an undercurrent, a sentiment that recurs in spoken and written expression without being thought out. It is necessary to bring it out, to articulate it in order to realise its contradictions. Essentially it assumes that anyone who comes from a particular background or place can be defined in the same way as anyone else who comes from the same background or place.

An examination of the variety and complexity of personal experience can illustrate the inadequacy of this simple idea of personal identity. Graham Crow and Graham Allan (1994), in their survey of community studies, acknowledged that you can have one place, but different communities, or rather different experiences of community: people might live in the same area as each other but experience that area differently.[8] Graham Day and Jonathan Murdoch (1993), in their study of the impact of social change on a rural South Wales valley, principally from migration into the valley, reported that people judged the changes in terms of the impact on their 'community', although their sense of unity did not correspond with a geographical unit. The villagers continually renegotiated their identity and sense of belonging.[9]

This process of renegotiation or reinvention of identity was observed in a different direction by Katy Gardner (1995) in her study of the patterns in people's migration from a village in the Sylhet area of North East Bangladesh. People crossed international boundaries in their migrations but continued to maintain close ties with their home village. From her study Katy Gardner concluded that migration involved a constant process of reinvention.[10]

The difficulty of seeking to define people's identities according to outside perceptions of who they are rather than accepting their own definitions was illustrated by David Donnison and Alan Middleton (1987) in their report on the GEAR project, which was set up in an attempt to revive the East End of Glasgow. They discovered people's own sense of who they were and from where they came, regardless of official categories and major social and economic change. In a survey people were asked to identify the part of Glasgow in which they lived. None described themselves as living in the GEAR area. Sixty percent denied categorically that they lived in the officially assigned areas. They identified themselves with traditional communities whose origins could be traced to the eighteenth century to villages which then lay outside the city of Glasgow.[11]

The social construction of self: as a more complex process

To imply that a person's identity and sense of self, can be determined directly and simply by his/her background is to attribute them to a single factor. They are 'socially constructed' in a simple direct way. Such a view is rarely articulated: rather it is a sentiment which underlies much expression. It is more likely that the idea that a person's identity and sense of self is socially constructed will be presented as a more complex process of interaction from childhood on: interaction with parents, with people who live in the same locality, or with groups and institutions, from friends and school outwards.

Benjamin Barber (1984) asserted that we were born with potential natures and could realise them only in society.[12] Anthony Giddens (1991) argued that the very young child was called into existence by the environment provided for him/her by his/her care-giver.[13] Nancy Rosenberg (1992) claimed that self originated through relationships and language.[14] Christopher Berry (1994), in discussing human nature, insisted that no meaningful separation could be made between humans and their specific culture.[15] Erving Goffmann (1961) concluded that "The self ... is not a property of the person to whom it is attributed, but dwells rather in the pattern of social control that is exerted in connection with the person by himself and those around him. This special kind of institutional arrangement does not so much support the self as constitute it." [16]

The belief that personal identity and self can arise only from a specific culture or from the social and economic structures within which the individual person lives and moves is reflected in another sense. It is reflected in a belief in the negative consequences of an absence of those factors of culture or social relationships or economic structures which – it is believed – help to nurture personal identity and a sense of self. It is reflected, for example, in a belief in the negative impact of urban life on relationships and personal identity and indeed on 'community'. This belief is evident especially in American thought. Robert E. Park (1925) referred to what he described as the disintegrating influence of city life and pointed to the influence of the urban environment as a cause for the breakdown of local attachments and the weakening of the primary group." [17] Louis Wirth (1938) accepted that social contacts in the city might still be face to face, but believed that they had become impersonal, superficial and transitory.[18] Norton E. Long (1986) dismissed American cities as economic sites for combining and recombining atoms.[19]

Such pessimistic views of human existence reflect a sense of the individual person as not so much an actor with at least some capacity to shape his/her social and cultural and economic environment as a reactor, reacting to and being shaped by the environment. Anthony Giddens (1991) – while acknowledging the creativity of the individual person in reacting to environment – emphasised what he described as the reflexive project of the self.[20]

Karl Marx, while rejecting the idea of a human nature inherent in each individual as being an abstraction from reality, did believe in the individuality of each person. Indeed he believed in a need to assert self. He proclaimed that "... communists ... are very well aware that egoism, just as much as self-sacrifice, is in definite circumstances a necessary form of the self-assertion of individuals." They sought "... the abolition of a state of things in which relationships become independent of individuals, in which individuality is subservient to chance ..." [21] Labour itself could be individual: "Supposing that we had produced in a human manner; each of us would in his production have doubly affirmed himself and his fellow men ... in that case our products would be like so many mirrors, out of which our essence shone." [22]

Nevertheless, for Marx individuality could emerge only in society and was determined essentially by social existence: "Man is ... not only a political animal, but an animal which can develop into an individual only in society ..." [23] Also: "... the human essence is ... in its reality ... the ensemble of social relations." [24]

The social construction of self: what it does not explain

Karl Marx expressed – more imaginatively than most of his followers – what I would describe as a thoroughly social sense of self. Individuality, personal identity, a sense of self emerge from culture, social existence, environment; no matter how dynamic the process of interaction is.

But there are some things which the social construction of self theory does not explain. I believe that the cases which are reported below raise doubts about the theory within its own terms of reference of concentrating on social existence. We see people who live in the same place but are strangers to each other. People invent and reinvent personal identity when faced with movement and social change. People react to unusual or extreme situations in quite unpredictable ways which are distinct from or even contrary to the common patterns of action within the cultural traditions or social networks from which they come or within which they live.

(a)

For example: Rosemary Harris (1972), in her study of a town in Northern Ireland divided between Catholic and Protestant residents, observed how people living in the same place can be both neighbours and strangers. She observed that, despite the extent to which people share a common culture, and the vast amount in common between households at the same economic level, that people's social lives were largely separate. Their social networks consisted overwhelmingly of their own co-religionists.[25]

(b)

It could be argued that in such a society people can be prisoners of a very specific and selective culture characterised by (in this example) religious attachment and belief and reinforced by kin networks and church, school and other meeting places. Therefore individuality, personal identity and self can be said to be socially constructed, but in a more specific and selective way, because each person's social networks (in this example) are based mostly on ties with his/her co-religionists rather than on ties with neighbours as such. However, such an interpretation, of people being prisoners of a very specific and selective culture, then has problems in coping with the idea of people inventing and reinventing personal identity, and the exercise of will which such a process represents. Katy Gardner's report (1995) on fifteen months field work with a village in the Sylhet area of North East Bangladesh and the patterns of migration from the village across international boundaries, emphasises this process of reinvention of identity as a response to migration.[26] Graham Day and Jonathan Murdoch (1993) reported on how residents of a rural valley in South Wales renegotiated their identities and their sense of belonging in response to actual or threatened change arising from migration into the valley and the consequent pressure on the housing market.[27]

(c)

If each person's identity and sense of self are 'socially constructed' can each person's behaviour and the choices he/she makes be predicted? The logic of a thoroughly social sense of self is that behaviour, reactions to particular situations should be predictable, given sufficient knowledge of each person's upbringing, cultural roots and social networks. And often in routine, everyday situations people may act or react according to the habits of upbringing or cultural conditioning or group interest. But how do people act or react in unusual or extreme situations, especially when confronted by issues of conscience or personal danger? Norman Geras (1995) surveyed research into those people who came to the rescue of Jews and other groups in Nazi Europe, and their motives as rescuers. He sought to examine to what degree rescue behaviour could be related to and predicted by the rescuer's background, whether in terms of social class and status, or political or religious belief, or parental influence or personality type. The consistent pattern in research findings was that there was a lack of pattern. For example, studies which suggested that the majority of rescuers were working class (as in Berlin) were qualified by studies which suggested that there was an even spread of rescuers according to class and professional status. Some rescuers were left-wing in their political affiliation or outlook, but the majority had no political affiliations. Many rescuers had strong religious beliefs and affiliations but many did not. Some rescuers were 'socially marginal' but many were not. And there was no one personality type represented among rescuers. Only two elements seemed to be common among rescuers. One element was that they were in a minority: a significant number of people provided rescue for Jews and other groups, but most people did not. The other element was that almost all rescuers admitted to universalist moral values as motives for their actions, whether or not their actions were underpinned by religious belief. Rescue of Jews, or other people fleeing Nazi persecution, required an act of will that could not be predicted according to upbringing or cultural conditioning or group interest.[28]

(d)

Usually rescue involved more than one rescuer. For example, it might involve family members working together. And by definition it involved close contact and a relationship with the person being rescued. But the act of rescue could not be predicted on the basis of the (would be) rescuers' background. How much less could an entirely solitary act of resistance be predicted on the basis of that person's background?

Gordon Zahn (1964) described the case of Franz Jagerstatter: born in 1907 in a small village in Upper Austria and executed in 1943 in a military prison in Berlin for refusal to do military service in the German Army; a refusal based on his opposition to the Nazi regime and to the war.[29]

Franz Jagerstatter was a small farmer who came from and lived most of his life in a settlement of one hundred or so households. He left school at fourteen years. He was not in his lifetime a public figure nor did he seek to be. Gordon Zahn noted that it was almost an accident that we knew anything at all about him. He took his stand in opposition to almost all of his fellow villagers and against the advice of his Church and his family. Gordon Zahn noted that Franz Jagerstatter stood completely alone in his rebellion.(p.61). How can that rebellion be explained? From where did Franz Jagerstatter come?

His rebellion was not rooted in culture and society. He came from a section of society and a part of his country which was conservative, rural and Catholic. Not only did it encourage a respect for authority, but also a certain sympathy for Nazism. Braunau, the birthplace of Adolf Hitler, was thirty kilometres away and the provincial capital of Linz was where Adolf Eichmann grew up.

His rebellion was not in response to any prompting from his Church. On the contrary: although Franz Jagerstatter was a very orthodox Catholic in belief and observance, he was out of step with the Church in his attitude to the Nazi regime and to the war. He referred to the Union of Austria and Germany as "the day the Austrian Church let herself be taken prisoner." (p.116). He complained that he did not know of one bishop who had opposed the war. The official church – his local pastor, other priests and his bishop – all advised him against the stand which he took.

And his rebellion was not sustained by any organised group or class. His wife confirmed that he was not in contact with anti-Nazi groups.

His rebellion was not in response to family influences or to social networks. His mother opposed his stand openly and his wife advised against it. Almost all the residents of St. Radegund, while expressing respect and liking for him as a person, rejected the stand he took. He was referred to by people he had known as "mentally deranged" for his stand. (p.151) It appears that he stopped going to the local inn so as to avoid the political arguments which followed.

His rebellion was not unthinking or without doubts. He recognised that he was following different norms from those around him. (p.181) and there is evidence that at a number of stages he felt severe difficulty in maintaining the stand that nevertheless he believed he must take.

Gordon Zahn sought an explanation for Franz Jagerstatter's rebellion in the theory of reference groups: the reference to the values and beliefs which past and future groups might be seen to embody. He noted that Franz Jagerstatter had a special interest in the saints and heroes of the early Church. (p.193) But such a theory cannot alter the argument that Franz Jagerstatter's rebellion was an exercise of real choice and a real act of will. Of course, it can be argued that his case was wholly exceptional and as such cannot sustain a particular view of personal identity and self. But an exceptional case can argue *against* a particular view of personal identity and self. I would argue that case of Franz Jaggerstatter argues against a thoroughly social sense of self. The exercise of choice and the act of will which his rebellion represented cannot be explained at all by reference to the upbringing, or cultural conditioning, or family or social networks, or political attachments or institutional influences into which he was born and in which he lived. The situation in which he found himself was not exceptional. How he judged it and reacted to it was.

(e)

At various times individual people may be conscious of the situations in which they find themselves being different from the situations of other people around them, and may express a sense of their own situations as being different not only in the particular details in which they may be different, but in the sense of difference in general. This idea, of difference in general, of the awareness of a self which is different as a whole rather than being a set of different experiences, may emerge from a variety of life situations whether ordinary and everyday or unusual and extreme. Alison James (1995), in her analysis of childhood perceptions, referred to the study by M. Bluebond-Langner and others (1991) with children suffering from cancer and the ways in which their situation marked them out from other people. It was not the particular details of how they were marked out that was most important to them – it was the idea of difference.[30] Stanley Cohen and Laurie Taylor (1978), in their study of what they called resistance to everyday life, discussed the establishment of identity in situations provoking resistance or escape: for example, prisoners "clearing small subjective spaces" for themselves within the prison system (p.20), or people who sought escape from the normal order of society in adventure and exploration. Their subject, they declared, was "self in spite of the structural order of society."[31]

(f)

However, being conscious of difference as a whole, being conscious of self, does not mean necessarily resistance or rejection or escape. Liz McShane (1993), in her report on self-help groups in Northern Ireland funded under the Community Support Programme, described a former resident with the Simon Resettlement Scheme in Larne who had moved into her own flat, and what having her own flat meant to her – "... When you're in your own flat you're in your own wee world and you bring friends into your world. They can't just walk into it." [32] People in this situation are seeking space, but it is not simply physical space they seek: it is their own space. Seeking it and achieving it is an act that not only indicates difference but also asserts difference; and in doing so asserts self.

(g)

Asserting difference, asserting self, may involve seeking a degree of privacy; and seeking a degree of privacy might be taken to represent an assertion of difference and of self. Privacy could be seen as an essential element in the idea of independent living. Jenny Morris (1993) reported on the reactions of people to life in residential institutions and the importance of achieving privacy. One (former) resident complained about sharing parts of your life with people with whom you have not chosen to live. Another resident looked forward to her own bungalow so that other people wouldn't know who was coming or going.[33] Alison Petch (1994), in a review of eleven supported accommodation projects across Scotland observed that for many of the residents it was not the houses or their specific locations which was important, but rather that they provided a source of security and privacy, often for the first time in a long while.[34]

Achieving privacy, securing one's own space, is not equivalent to withdrawal or rejection of association. Rather it is a necessary element in people's lives and a necessary stage of development. Martin Bulmer (1986), in his account of the work of Philip Abrams and his team on neighbours and neighbouring, reported that respect for privacy was identified consistently by people featured in their studies as an enormously valued component of positive neighbouring.[35] Alan Tyne (1992), reporting on case studies of success in integration, described the case of Susan who had lived in an institutional world for women who had been and were violent, but who was helped over time to settle successfully in her own flat and make her own life. Having her own place contributed towards Susan developing relationships and a sense of self worth: she discovered that she could make a contribution to the lives of people around her.[36]

The self and others: what is distinctive?

All this suggests that there is some element of discontinuity between each person and his/her background: between each person and other people. But this distinctiveness of the individual person, of the individual self does not need to be explained as a separation from or rejection of forms of association with other people. It does not require the erection of exclusive boundaries between people. What is the essence of this distinction between the individual person and other people, between the self and the world? Mary Midgley (1994) pointed to an answer in her discussion of human freedom. She asserted that what was distinctive about human freedom was an individual's ability to act, in spite of many inner divisions, as a whole. But this unity as individuals was not "something given" – it was a continuing lifelong project.[37]

Mary Midgley illustrated this distinctive wholeness of the individual person by putting forward the case of Evan Jones, a miner. Evan Jones is a miner recovered from serious illness. He ought to have died two years before, but he defied the judgement of the doctors in a case of spontaneous remission. And he is not simply alive: he is active in the affairs of his village. There was, Mary Midgley suggested, various ways of explaining his recovery: in medical science, in relation to Evan Jones' illness and physical condition; in genetics; in relation to his family history; in geography; in relation to local climate and conditions. Explanation could be sought also in general labour and housing conditions, in wars and in national politics; or in local institutions and culture.

But although these means of enquiry might explain a great deal about Evan Jones' general situation they would offer little explanation as to why his response differed from other people's responses: "... To explain this we need to know him in the ordinary but very significant personal sense ...[We shall have to] see him as an individual, taking in his own point of view and that of those people nearest to him." [38]

The self: Do we start with nothing? Is what we become or what we are pre-determined?

If we do not accept that there is this distinctiveness of the individual self; if we do not accept that there is a discontinuity between the individual person and other people; if we believe that what we are is what we have become through a process of interaction with other people and our own environment – then we must consider the question: do we start at the very beginning with nothing? Does each person at their beginning as an infant experience the world, to quote William James, as a "booming, buzzing confusion" ? [39]

Mary Midgley (1995) rejected any suggestions that the individual person is indeterminate and plastic at birth, or that the newly arrived infant is a kind of blank paper. But if we start with something rather than nothing, what do we start with? [40]

We may start with a capacity for language. Stephen Crain (1993) acknowledged that most linguists have reached the conclusion that "at least some properties of human language are innately determined." [41] Stephen Pinker (1994) believed that the universality of complex language suggested a universal instinct for language. He reported on the studies of Joseph Greenberg and later analysts who identified hundreds of universal patterns in languages around the world.[42]

Stephen Pinker argued that all infants come into the world with linguistic skills. He described studies which illustrated the capacities of children not merely to 'acquire' but to invent and reinvent languages. Examples were 'creole' languages, which represented the standardisations of 'pidgin' language and expressions; and sign languages and expressions.[43] He proposed that a capacity for complex language was universal because children demonstrated that capacity by reinventing complex language generation after generation – "... they just can't help it ..." Children, he considered, deserved most of the credit for the languages they acquired.[44]

For Stephen Pinker, the universal patterns underlying language led to conclusions about the physiology of the brain: they suggested "a commonality in the brains of speakers." This commonality in the brain's capacities for language could be seen in a different sense, in the impact of several different kinds of neurological and genetic impairments which compromised the capacity for language, but which spared other capacities for understanding and learning.[45]

We may start with a capacity for language; we may start also with a capacity for music. Patricia Gray, Bernie Krause, Jelle Atema, Roger Payne, Carol Krumhansl and Luis Baptista argued in *Science* (2001) that the fact that music making was found in all human cultures suggested that there is a deep human need to create, perform and listen to music. They considered it possible that human beings may have been making music for several hundred thousand years.

But music may have even deeper roots. Patricia Gray and her colleagues reported striking similarities between the undersea songs of hump-back whales and human music making. The songs of hump-back whales were strikingly similar to human compositions in relation to rhythms; musical phrases; musical intervals; and a mixture of percussive, noisy elements with relatively pure tones that is similar to that used in Western symphonic music. In addition, hump-back songs contain repeating refrains that form rhymes. The whales may use rhyme in the same way as humans do: to help them remember complex material.[46]

These arguments about language and music are examples of the general argument that what we are is what we start with as well as what we become; and we start, for example, with our genes (See Chapter 4 and Appendix A). Philip Kitcher (1996) considered it a commonplace of genetics that the majority of traits of any organism – including human beings – resulted from

the action of many genes and the interaction between the developing organism and its environment.[47]
Thomas Bouchard (1997) considered that genes were likely to make a given body or personality more likely to respond to its environment in certain ways.[48]

Of course it is possible to promote a genetic or biological determinism instead of or alongside a social determinism: to argue that human behaviour or personality are determined by our genes. But as noted above (Chapter 4), few people argue for this position even when emphasising the critical importance of our genes. Walter Gilbert, for example, complained of what he described as a "shallow determinism." [49] Richard Dawkins (1982) observed that there was no general reason for expecting genetic influences to be any more irreversible that environmental ones.[50]

I have argued above that the logic of a thoroughly social sense of self is that behaviour or reactions to particular situations should be predictable given sufficient knowledge of each person's upbringing, cultural roots and social networks. Equally if human nature is determined by our genes, if social behaviour is a product of evolution, if we inherit at least a predisposition to certain behaviours because our genes have programmed them for us – then who we are, where and with whom we belong and how we behave should be predictable given sufficient knowledge of each person's genetic structure.

But lack of predictability is a reality of our behaviour as is predictability. This is as true of genetic influences as it is of cultural and social influences. Research studies have failed to link specific human behaviours to solitary genes or small sets of genes (see Chapter 4), and have suggested rather that the majority of traits of any organism, including human beings, resulted from many genes acting indirectly and often quite subtly, and interacting with the environment.

Studies of identical twins, who are born with exactly the same genes when the fertilised egg splits in half, have demonstrated both the power of genes to shape human behaviour and personality traits, and the limits of that power. As well as behaving and reacting to situations in similar ways and demonstrating similar personality traits, pairs of identical twins have demonstrated differences (see Chapter 4). Sharing the same genes has not meant that identical twins have behaved always in the same way or demonstrated the same personality traits.

An outstanding example of the pitfalls of genetic determinism and predictability has been the area of race. Stephen Pinker (1994) pointed out that eighty five per cent of human genetic variations consist of the differences between one person and another within the same ethnic group, tribe or nation. Only eight per cent are between different ethnic groups. Only seven per cent are between different 'races'.[51] Jonathan Marks (1995) also recognised that the biological differences between races are minimal. Race is a social or cultural or historical category rather than a biological one.[52] The reality of our attachments and associations is one of biodiversity and lack of predictability.

Genetic determinism and predictability, as with social determinism and predictability, contradict the reality of human choice. There is an element of real choice in human actions and interactions (see Chapter 4). For example, we can and do face and are conscious of facing real conflicts of value within ourselves and between ourselves and other people about what to do in certain situations. We can, therefore, make real choices: that is, we can choose to act differently; and in some situations some people choose to act in one way while other people, facing the same situations, choose to act in another way.

As I have argued above in Chapter 4, the influence of our genes is important but not all important. People can and sometimes do act differently from what might appear to be predicted by environment and upbringing. And people can and sometimes do act differently from what might appear to be predicted by their genetic structures. And when they act differently, they may be choosing consciously to act differently.

The self: unique awareness and unique existence

So we may return to the theme that there is some element of discontinuity between each person and his/her background: an inescapable distinction between the individual person and other people; an inescapable distinction, therefore, between the individual person and the community.

Individuality, personal identity, a sense of self cannot be explained simply in terms of environment or culture or social existence. Nor can they be explained simply in terms of particular genes or the genetic structure of each person. The limitations of such explanations, the questions which they do not answer, suggest that there is for each person a very personal, almost private existence. Sometimes there may be a dimension of unique existence.

Unique existence does not mean separate existence, as Robert Nozick (1974) described it when he insisted on "... the fact of our separate existences." [53] However existence is described, each person's existence consists of many facts, some to do with that person by himself/herself, some to do with that person's connection to/interaction with other people (see Chapter 4).

The facts of a person's existence can be considered as the facts of existence which are specific to that person. Unique existence refers both to facts of existence which are unique to a particular person and also to that person's awareness of their uniqueness. Unique existence can be seen in the sometimes solitary adventure of scientific enquiry. The poet William Wordsworth painted a vivid picture of this dimension of unique existence with his words on Isaac Newton, after contemplating a marble bust of the great scientist:

> *The marble index of a mind*
> *Forever voyaging through strange seas of thought*
> *Alone.* [54]

A scientist can accept and may indeed welcome this particular solitude of enquiry and discovery without being a recluse. Richard Feynman was awarded the Nobel Prize for Physics in 1965 for his work on quantum electrodynamics. Between 1943 and 1945 when he was in his mid-twenties he worked at Los Alamos on the Manhattan Project – the design and construction of the first atomic bombs. He was described then by Robert Oppenheimer as "the most brilliant young physicist here." From 1945 to 1950 he was Professor of Physics at Cornell University and from 1950 until his death in 1988 he was Professor of Physics at the California Institute of Technology. In the 1980's he became a public figure through television programmes and the publishing of two volumes of anecdotes and observations about his life and science. In 1986 he accepted an invitation to chair the U.S. presidential commission investigating the Challenger space shuttle disaster.

Richard Feynman was one of the outstanding intellects in his field. Roger Penrose (1998) – himself a leading physicist – considered him to be one of the twentieth century's outstanding theoretical physicists.[55] John Gribbin and Mary Gribbin (1998) considered him to be "the greatest physicist of his generation." [56]

Richard Feynman was not a reclusive academic who struggled to communicate with people outside his own field. He demonstrated a rare talent for communication, firstly as a celebrated lecturer and storyteller and eventually through television programmes and popular books. Freeman Dyson (1998) wrote that he never saw him (Feynman) give a lecture that did not make people laugh.[57] Roger Penrose (1998) considered that Feynman enjoyed being centre-stage and was undoubtedly a showman. He referred to him as "this streetwise New Yorker." [58] Yet Richard Feyman could discuss the experience of scientific enquiry by referring to the "wonderful loneliness of discovery." [59]

A person may travel, in thought or to other places, to achieve this solitude. But it may also be a natural dimension of everyday existence. A friend said to me once that there were things about her which everybody knew and things about her which only some people knew and things about her which no one else would ever know. Could this statement be true about some other people, or true about people in general? It is a statement which cannot be proven, in relation to any person making it, by established means of observation and recording. Each person will know whether or not this statement applies to himself/herself. But he/she cannot prove for other people that this statement represents a truth about himself/herself. Each person can only affirm that it is true: by definition, anyone making such a statement is referring to things about himself/herself that he/she does not choose to make known to anyone else. So not only may there be facts of a person's existence which are unique to that person: there may be also an awareness of those facts which is unique to that person because it is not shared by anyone else.

Either you deny unique existence and justify that denial; or you accept unique existence and seek to explain it. And if there is unique existence, then there is for particular, individual persons a dimension of existence and an awareness of existence which is not and cannot be included within the boundaries of the groups or associations – or 'communities' – to which those persons are attached or with which they are involved.

REFERENCES

1. COHEN, Anthony. (1994). *Self-consciousness : an alternative anthropology of identity*. London; New York: Routledge. p.73

2. WILLIAMS, Raymond. (1983). *Keywords*. London: Flamingo; Fontana. p.76

3. QUILLET, Jeannine. (1988). Community, counsel and representation, *The Cambridge history of medieval political thought*. Edited by J.H. Burns. Cambridge: Cambridge University Press. p.521

4. *INTERNATIONAL encyclopedia of the social sciences*. (1986). Vol.14. [New York]: Macmillan; The Free Press. p.152

5. BERGER, Peter, and LUCKNOW, Thomas. (1978). *The social construction of reality*. Harmondsworth: Penguin; Peregrine. pp.13, 194

6. ROSENBERG, Nancy (editor). (1992). *The Japanese sense of self.* Cambridge: Cambridge University Press. p.3

7. SIBLEY, David. (1995). *The Geography of exclusion*. London: Routledge. p.7

8. ALLAN, Graham, and CROW, Graham. (1994). *Community life : an introduction to local social relations*. Hemel Hempstead: Harvester Wheatsheaf. p.157

9. DAY, Graham, and MURDOCH, Jonathan. (1993). Loyalty and community, *Sociological Review* (London: Routledge & Kegan Paul). Vol.41, no.1. p.94

10. GARDNER, Katy. (1995). *Global migrants, local lives : travel and transformation in rural Bangladesh.* Oxford: OUP. Preface

11. DONNISON, David, and MIDDLETON, Alan. 1987). *Regenerating the inner city : Glasgow's experience.* London: Routledge & Kegan Paul. p.15

12. BARBER, Benjamin. (1984). *Strange democracy : participatory politics for a new age.* Berkeley, CA: University of California Press. p.89

13. GIDDENS, Anthony. (1991). *Modernity and self-identity : self and society in the late modern age.* Cambridge: Polity. pp.39, 52

14. ROSENBERG, Nancy (editor). (1992). *The Japanese sense of self.* p.67

15. BERRY, Christopher J. (1993). Human nature, *The Blackwell dictionary of 20th century political thought.* pp.268-269

16. GOFFMANN, Erving. (1961). Inpatients please, *Asylums.* Harmondsworth: Penguin. p.154

17. PARK, Robert E ... [et al]. (1925). *The city.* Chicago, Ill: University of Chicago Press. Reprinted 1974. pp.24-25

18. WIRTH, Louis. (1938). Urbanism as a way of life, *American Journal of Sociology.* Quoted in: Urbanism and kinship bonds : a test of four generalizations, by Thomas C. Wilson, *Social Forces* (Chapel Hill, NC: University of North Carolina Press). Vol.71, no.3 (March 1993). pp.703-712

19. LONG, Norton E. (1986). The city as a political community, *Journal of Community Psychology* (Brandon, VT: Clinical Psychology Publishing Corporation). Vol.14, no.1. p.72

20. GIDDENS, Anthony. (1991). *Modernity and self-identity.* pp.5 etc.

21. MARX, Karl, and ENGELS, Friedrich. (1932). The German ideology, *Karl Marx : selected writings.* Edited by David McLellan. Oxford: OUP, 1977. pp.183, 190

22. MARX, Karl. (18--). On James Mill, *Karl Marx : selected writings.* pp.121-122

23. MARX, Karl. (18--). General introduction to *Grundrisse, Karl Marx : selected writings.* p.346

24. Marx, Karl. (18--). Theses on Feuerbach, *Karl Marx : selected writings.* p.157

25. HARRIS, Rosemary. (1972). *Prejudice and tolerance in Ulster*. Manchester: Manchester University Press. Introductory preface

26. GARDNER, Katy. (1995). *Global migrants, local lives*. pp. vii, 1

27. DAY, Graham, and MURDOCH, Jonathan. (1993). Locality and community, *Sociological Review* (London: Routledge & Kegan Paul). Vol.41, no.1. p.84

28. GERAS, Norman. (1995). Richard Rorty and the righteous among nations, *Journal of Applied Philosophy* (Abingdon: Carfax). Vol.12, no.2. pp.151

29. ZAHN, Gordon. (1966). *In solitary witness : the life and death of Franz Jaggerstatter*. London: Geoffrey Chapman

30. JAMES, Alison. (1995). On being a child, *Questions of consciousness*. Edited by Anthony Cohen and Nigel Rapport. London: Routledge. p.63

31. COHEN, Stanley, and TAYLOR, Laurie. (1978). *Escape attempts : the theory and practice of resistance to everyday life*. Harmondsworth: Pelican. p.23

32. McSHANE, Liz. (1993). *Community support : a pilot programme*. Belfast: Northern Ireland Voluntary Trust. p.55

33. MORRIS, Jenny. (1993). *Independent lives : community care and disabled people*. Basingstoke: Macmillan. pp.62-63

34. PETCH, Alison. (1994). The best move I've ever made : the role of housing for those with mental health problems, *Caring for people in the community : the new welfare*. Edited by Michael Titterton. London: Jessica Kingsley. p.82

35. BULMER, Martin. (1986). *Neighbours*. Cambridge: Cambridge University Press. p.30

36. TYNE, Alan. (1992). Normalisation : from theory to practice, *Normalisation : a reader for the nineties*. Edited by Hilary Brown and Helen Smith. London: Tavistock; Routledge. p.36

37. MIDGLEY, Mary. (1994). *The ethical primate*. London; New York: Routledge. pp.18-22

38. *ibid*. pp.63-64

39. JAMES, William. (Late 19th–early 20th C). Quoted in: The social construction of self, by Kenneth J. Gergen, *The self : psychological and philosophical issues*. Edited by Theodore Mischel. Oxford: OUP, 1977. p.141

40. MIDGLEY, Mary. (1995). *Beast and man*. Revised edition. London: Routledge. p. xxix

41. CRAIN, Stephen. (1993). Language acquisition in the absence of experience, *Language acquisition : core readings.* Edited by Paul Bloom. Hemel Hempstead: Harvester Wheatsheaf. p.365

42. PINKER, Steven. (1994). *The language instinct.* Harmondsworth: Penguin. p.233

43. *ibid.* pp.33-39

44. *ibid.* p.40

45. *ibid.* p.41

46. GRAY, Patricia M ... [et al]. (2001). The music of nature and the nature of music, *Science* (Washington, DC). Vol.291 (5th January 2001). pp.52-54

47. KITCHER, Philip. (1996). *Lives to come : the genetic revolution and human possibilities.* London: Allen Lane. Penguin. p.60

48. BOUCHARD, Thomas. (1997). Whenever the twain shall meet, *The sciences* (New York: New York Academy of Sciences). Sept.-Oct. 1997. p.56

49. GILBERT, Walter. (1992). A vision of the Grail, *The code of codes : scientific and social issues in the Human Genome Project.* Edited by Daniel J. Kevles and Leroy Hoo. Cambridge, MS: Harvard University Press. p.96

50. DAWKINS, Richard. (1982). *The extended phenotype.* Oxford: OUP. p.13

51. PINKER, Steven. (1994). *The language instinct.* p.430

52. MARKS, Jonathan. (1995). *Human biodiversity : genes, race and history.* New York: Aldine de Gruyter. p.274

53. NOZICK, Robert. (1974). *Anarchy, state and utopia.* Oxford: Blackwell. p.33

54. WORDSWORTH, William. Quoted in: *Isaac Asimov's Biographical encyclopedia of science and technology.* London: Pan, 1975. p.141

55. PENROSE, Roger. (1998). Introduction, *Six not-so-easy pieces*, by Richard Feynman. London: Allen Lane; Penguin. 1998. p. vii

56. GRIBBIN, John, and GRIBBIN, Mary. (1998). *Richard Feynman : a life in science.* London: Penguin. p.283

57. DYSON, Freeman. (1998). Quoted in: *Richard Feynman : a life in science.* p. xiv

58. PENROSE, Roger. (1998). Introduction, *Six not-so-easy pieces*, by Richard Feynman. pp. viii, x

59. FEYNMAN, Richard. (1988). *What do you care what other people think?*. London: University Paperbacks. p.72

Part 4:

Conclusions

12

UNHELPFUL APPLICATIONS OF THE IDEA OF COMMUNITY

Unitary community – Identifying community with physical space – A thoroughly social sense of self – As a link to and as a metaphor for other ideas

Unhelpful applications of the idea of community: unitary community

The unitary idea of community is expressed in a sense of wholeness in thinking about community and society. In political philosophy it is expressed in the belief that all of a particular society – state and people, governors and governed – are part of a whole.

In social policy it is expressed as an assumption that if people have common characteristics, e.g. if they are resident in the same place, or come from the same cultural or religious or ethnic background, or if they share personal problems or interests, then they represent parts of a whole.

The unitary idea of community may be an underlying assumption in ideas about rehabilitation within or integration with the community. Rehabilitation and integration are common themes in services and activities which are intended to help people who experience obstacles – such as physical disabilities or learning disabilities – which can affect their capacity or their opportunities to participate fully in society (see Part 1, Chapter 2).

The therapeutic community (Part 1, Chapter 2) could be said to represent for some people an image of a unitary community. The therapeutic community is an invented form of association both for people who are in the same situation or who face the same problems as each other, and also for those professionals seeking to work with them.

References to the community and to the local community in area regeneration programmes, whether they are directed at poverty or unemployment or urban decline or rural underdevelopment, often imply a cohesive or unitary view of how people of a particular area may think and act and interact (see Part 1, Chapter 2).

But not everyone identifies with the 'whole community'; not everyone wants to be part of the 'community'. Some people may not fit in with the prevailing values, attitudes or forms of association of a given society at a particular point of time (Part 3, Chapter 10). Some people may seek alternative forms of association to those which are immediately available to them. Some people may seek support or friendship in smaller groups at the margins or in the corners of the society in which they live, with people who face similar concerns or circumstances as themselves. And some people may want simply to 'keep themselves to themselves' (Part 3, Chapter 11).

A unitary idea of community is not helpful to the development of social policy if it encourages assumptions that what is good for the people of a particular area or group as a whole is equally relevant to and good for all the smaller groups and individuals within that area or larger group. Such assumptions deny differences between people as to what they need and what they want (see Part 1, Chapter 2).

Sometimes it may be an appropriate objective for helping services to encourage a separate or at least a distinct group consciousness among some people as a means of promoting their self esteem. Sometimes it may be an appropriate means of helping people to encourage deliberately a variety of forms of association, a variety of communities, rather than one all embracing community to which it is supposed to be desirable for everyone to belong (Part 1, Chapter 2).

Unhelpful applications of the idea of community: identifying community with physical space

Often in social policy reports, statements or debates there is an instinctive presumption that locality and physical proximity in themselves may give a special quality to or may extend or deepen relationships. For example, it was seen in the report of the House of Commons Social Services Committee (1985), which expressed a preference for local services over distant services as an element in defining community care (see Part 1, Chapter 1); or in the Cumberledge Report on Community Nursing (1986), which proposed that nursing services should be organised locally and which called for neighbourhood nursing services (Part 1, Chapter 1). This presumption was seen in the Griffiths Report (1988), with its emphasis on caring for people "... in the community where they and their families have lived" and on locating responsibility for care "... as near to the individual and carer as possible"; and in its characterisation of institutional care in terms of large size and physical remoteness and segregation (Part 1, Chapter 1).

The presumption of a link between locality or physical proximity and relationships is seen also in area regeneration programmes, in the emphasis on the supposed benefit of having offices or bases for providing services located close to people (see Part 1, Chapter 3).

But to pursue a simple preference for near at hand over far away, for closeness over distance, for large scale over small scale leaves an insoluble problem. That problem is: where is the physical dividing line to be drawn which marks the point at which the negative physical relationship becomes the positive physical relationship? At which point does negative or excessive distance become positive closeness; or excessive large scale become positive small scale; or negative segregation become positive openness? (How many gates do you have to open or how many walls do you have to demolish?)

The difficulties created by an assumption of physical space in itself as a factor in relationships was highlighted by John McKnight's complaint about people living 'in the community' without relationships, while being surrounded by 'community' services (see Part1, Chapter 1); and by Hilary Brown's and Helen Smith's description of people being segregated "in ones and twos in private spaces." (see Part 1, Chapter 1)

I would argue that it is not physical distance or size or location in themselves which are the important factors in determining opportunities for people to participate in a range of social relationships. Rather it is the access to contact with other people which is open to each person; the degree of autonomy which each person is able to exercise in making choices; the existing relationships in which each person is involved and on which he or she can build; and the perception which each person has of his or her circumstances and what he or she may be able to do to change them.

Unhelpful applications of the idea of community: a thoroughly social sense of self

What I would describe as a thoroughly social sense of self is one which sees individual personal identity as emerging from and being determined by social existence, culture and environment. What we are is what we have become through a process of interaction with other people and with our environment. A thoroughly social sense of self means defining a person in terms of their attachments to and association with other people, past and present. So to say that someone belongs to, is part of a community is an example of defining that person in terms of their attachments to and associations with other people.

But a thoroughly social sense of self does not acknowledge the variety and complexity of what people want for themselves and what they experience, and how they perceive their experience. Different people experience the same thing differently. People may live in the same area, or have something else in common, and be conscious of what they have in common. They may know each other. They may describe themselves as being part of the community of A...; but each person does not necessarily experience the same community as each other person (Part 3, Chapter 11).

A thoroughly social sense of self should mean that people's behaviour and reactions to a particular situation should be predictable, given sufficient knowledge of each person's upbringing, cultural roots and social networks. It implies that people will act or react according to the habits of upbringing or cultural conditioning or group interest. But although people may react according to those habits in routine or everyday situations, they may react differently in unusual or extreme circumstances (Part 3, Chapter 11).

A thoroughly social sense of self does not come to terms with the distinctiveness of the individual person. There is an inescapable distinction between the individual person and other people; a distinction which is quite different from separation or rejection of forms of association with other people (part 3, Chapter 11). For example, the ideas of independent living represent an assertion of difference: an assertion of self. A degree of privacy can be seen as an essential element in the idea of independent living (see Part 3, Chapter 11).

A thoroughly social sense of self can encourage the idea that we start with nothing. If what we are is what we have become through a process of interaction with other people and with our environment, then perhaps at the very beginning as infants we start with nothing except for a few reflexes and an ability to learn. But such a view of human experience reflects a sense of the individual person as not so much an actor, with some capacity to shape his or her social and cultural and economic environment, as a re-actor, reacting to and being shaped by his or her environment. And it takes only social existence as its terms of reference in interpreting human experience and what and who we are. Such a view is surely unreasonable in the light of our present and developing understanding of genetics, and the capacities with which we are born: for example, our capacity for complex language or music. It is evident that what we are is what we start with as well as what we become (see Part 3, Chapter 11 and Part 2, Chapter 4).

Unhelpful applications of the idea of community: as a link to and as a metaphor for other ideas

The idea of community is used regularly as a link to and as a metaphor for other ideas: communication between people and government and other agencies: accountability by government and other outside agencies to people who are affected by their decisions; consultation with people about decisions which affect them; participation by people in the decision making process;

partnership between people and other outside agencies; self help activities by people experiencing problems.

The 'community' comes to represent all those people with whom government and other outside agencies should communicate; to whom they should be accountable, with whom they should consult, whom they should help to participate, with whom they should work in partnership. Or it may be taken to represent people who are seeking to help themselves through co-operative activity.

Commonly area regeneration programmes are supposed to depend for success on support from and involvement from 'local communities', and they may be criticised for their record in this respect (see Part 1, Chapter 3). For example, the official evaluation report on the Belfast Action Teams Programme commended the teams for being based on the ground among the communities they were seeking to assist. On the other hand, an independent review of the Making Belfast Work Programme, which took over the Belfast Action Teams, criticised the programme because "it had no mechanism for community involvement ... to allow communities to articulate needs and influence projects" (see Part 1, Chapter 3).

The use of the term 'community' in these contexts suggests again the unitary idea of community. To ask simply that government and other agencies communicate with the community, be accountable to the community or consult with the community implies that whoever the people are who are being referred to are all together, they are part of a whole. Their needs, and the appropriate responses to them, can be defined in the same standard way. But who are the community? Are we referring to the same people each time that we use the term? Is it the same people each time that government and other agencies are communicating with, or are accountable to or are consulting with or are helping to participate? If we are referring to different people each time that we use the term 'community' we should ask: is it necessary to use the term at all? Its continued use may obscure meaning and may obstruct clear assessments and statements of who governments and other agencies should be accountable to, who should be consulted, or who should be helped to participate, and how these purposes should be achieved. Use of the term 'community' may seem to cover everything when in reality it may explain nothing about who and how.

I would propose that the themes of communication, accountability, consultation, participation and self-help should be developed directly as tools for analysing activities, services and decision making structures rather than wrapping them up always in the idea of community. (Who should communicate with whom? Who should associate with whom in a process of self-help?). For me, these themes relate to the central issue of power – power in and over people's lives, and the decision making processes which affect them. Often, I believe, it is more useful to talk about power rather than about community. We should talk less about community and more about power and relationships.

13

THREE HELPFUL APPLICATIONS OF THE IDEA OF COMMUNITY

As an idea of limited applicability – As representing common interests, interactions, association – As being dynamic

Helpful applications of the idea of community: as an idea of limited applicability

I would argue that community is an idea of limited applicability. It is one of a number of ideas which may be useful in understanding relationships or developing services or planning programmes of intervention. Community is concerned with common interests, interaction and association between people outside of personal relationships and individualised, one to one relationships.

(I would define personal relationships as those relationships which you have with other persons who are important to you in themselves, not simply because they are part of a group or association which happens to be important to you, or because they have some function or provide some service which is important to you. Obviously you may have personal relationships in the above sense with parents or family or particular friends or partners. Personal relationships may develop within a group or association and because of the group or association).

Community represents one process of conscious interaction between people, but only one. Many helping relationships do not involve any process which might be described as a process of community. For example, most services or programmes under the heading of community care involve individualised, one to one helping relationships which are on too small a scale to justify the application of the term community to them (see Part 1, Chapters 1 & 2); and area regeneration programmes are likely to involve some essentially individualised services which again do not justify the application of the word 'community' to them (see Part 1, Chapter 3).

Helpful applications of the idea of community: as representing common interests, interactions, association

If community means anything, it refers to our social relationships and our social existence. Raymond Plant (1974) described community as "a highly contested meaning which we place upon the complexity of our social experience." I would propose that normally community can be taken to include the following elements:

- common interests among a group of people, and recognition by them of those common interests
- conscious interaction between and association among people with common interests
- some degree of common action and/or common organisation by them
- a sense of personal identification with the group as a whole by people within it.

I would argue that the idea of community should not be introduced if those elements are not present in a situation, and should be introduced only in as much as they are present to a significant degree.

Sometimes 'community' could be applied to small groups of people who share particular concerns and problems. Sometimes it could be applied to people who are scattered over different localities, perhaps even across international boundaries.

Above all, community implies relationships: types of relationship and qualities of relationship. I do not believe that it should be used simply because people happen to have something in common: for example, they are resident in the same areas, or they come from a similar background or they face the same changes to their environment, such as housing development or transport projects or other social or economic or institutional changes. Often when we use the word 'community' we encourage an assumption that we are describing the situation of a particular group of people when we may be failing to identify who we are talking about, or consider how they see themselves or what their relationships are with each other.

If the elements of common interests, conscious interaction and association are present to a significant degree within a particular group of people then it may be appropriate to talk about community because it may help to explain the relationships between these people. But it will be more realistic to accept the idea of community as one way of thinking about relationships between people; and to define community as a process of interaction or as a pattern of relationships which *sometimes* can provide a framework for relating to people in order to pursue the objectives of services or of programmes of intervention.

Helpful applications of the idea of community: as being dynamic

In as much as it may be a useful idea, I would argue that 'community' should be seen as a process of conscious interaction between people and as patterns of relationships which develop, rather than as particular social units. It is not realistic to discuss community, or a particular group of people who are supposed to constitute a community, as if they have a fixed pattern of relationships, which remains within clearly defined boundaries.

The idea of community which emerged from Graham Day's and Jonathan Murdoch's study of the Ithon Valley in Mid Wales (1993) was neither static nor unchanging. They concluded that it was processes of interaction between people which gave rise to "specific notions of community and locality" (see Part 2, Chapter 3 and Part 3, Chapter 5). Peter Willmott drew on various neighbourhood studies to demonstrate that people's sense of community was not unchanging. It was influenced substantially by their participation in social networks; and the length of time that they were resident in a particular place was a key factor in determining their participation in social networks (Part 2, Chapter 5). Katy Gardner, in her study of a village in North East Bangladesh and migration from it, observed how people's sense of who and what they were could change as they migrated. There was a constant process of reinvention (Part 3, Chapter 11).

It follows from this idea of community as being dynamic that it cannot be assumed in advance that particular patterns of relationships exist among a certain group of people simply because they have something in common (*e.g.* they are all resident in a certain locality). And it cannot be assumed in advance that if particular patterns of relationships existed at one time that they will remain unchanged for later times. People change, relationships develop, people move.

This idea of community as being dynamic has been expressed most vividly in Martin Buber's *Between Man and Man* ... "Community is where community happens." (English translation. Collins/Fontana, 1973. p.51)

14

TWO WAYS IN WHICH SOCIAL POLICY MAY MAKE USE OF THE IDEA OF COMMUNITY

Community as a framework for relating to people – Community as a process of offering or giving support

Community as a framework for relating to people

Community may offer a framework for social policy through which support is offered to people or services are organised. It may offer a framework through which ideas are expressed about social relationships and the problems people have in society.

Social policy is a body of ideas about how society is and how it ought to be, and what should be done to change it, and who should do it (see Appendix A: What is Social Policy?).. Social policy means judgements about the situation of particular people or particular groups of people in society and what can or should be done to change their situation. Social policy judgements may mean encouraging particular people or groups of people to do certain things. (They may mean also imposing restraints on what other people may do).

The state or local government agencies, or private charities, or local voluntary groups and other forms of association, may have these ideas about how society is and how it ought to be. They may make judgements about the situation (some) people are in and seek to do something about it. They may develop programmes of intervention: they may go into people's lives, encourage people to do things. They may offer resources including grants to groups and individuals.

Who are the people who are the subjects of social policies? What do they have in common? They may be, for example, all the people who are resident in an area which is a local or regional unit of national government. They may be the people who are resident in a particular area which has been selected as the subject of an aid programme because of a supposed concentration of problems (see Part 1, Chapter 3).

Or they may not live in the same area, but may be simply people who share a problem or conditions or need and may, it is supposed, be able to benefit from a particular service. Many health services, for example, represent a response to needs or problems which are not connected to locality.

People who are the subjects of social policies may be at certain stages of life, for which certain services are considered necessary, for example: education services or pensions or many health and welfare services for older people. Or they may be people who are having to cope with enforced changes such as unemployment and retraining, or moving house, or major illness, or disability.

How can agencies and organisations make contact with and relate to people who are subjects of social policies? How can they put ideas across, or offer services and resources? How can they identify what is relevant to people's lives?

If a group of people who are the subject of social policy are not simply an aggregate of individuals – if there is association, recognition of common interests and common action between them – then the idea of community may be relevant to the process of relating to them. It may help in seeking to understand them by understanding what they have in common which is part of what and who they are (see Part 3, Chapter 11).

And it may help in relating to people to become involved with their organisations, institutions, forms of association and informal networks.

But there are certain qualifications to the relevance of the idea of community as a framework for social policy – the idea of community goes only so far (see Part 3):

Firstly: the idea of community cannot be taken to mean fixed membership of a group nor fixed boundaries around a place/locality (see Part 2, Chapter 5). Therefore it cannot indicate everybody who is relevant to a social policy nor all of the area which is relevant to that social policy.

Secondly: there are people who do not 'belong' to a community or to one community (see Part 2, Chapter 5 ; Part 3, Chapters 9 and 10). All or most people are involved in a variety of groups, associations, networks or situations. Perhaps their involvements are many, or perhaps a few. Perhaps they are involved deeply, or perhaps they are involved only marginally. But the realities of social existence, the variety and complexity of social relationships mean that you cannot summarise people in one package. There is no such thing as 'the community'.

Thirdly: it is not realistic to define a certain community and say that 'X' belongs to it, so that relating to that community means that you are relating to 'X'. There is more than one approach to relating to 'X' and there is more than one approach to relating to the people who may be identified with that community (see Part 1, Chapter 2 ; Part 3, Chapter 6). So if any person or any organisation says, for example, that they are adopting a 'community development' approach in seeking to tackle certain problems or achieve social policy objectives, they can be asked: "That's good, but what other approaches are you trying?"

Community as a process of offering or giving support

'Community' may refer to one process in the development of helping relationships. This process may emerge when individualised helping relationships (helping relationships which focus on individual persons or family groups as in social casework or counselling) develop into a pattern of helping based on mutual support and the promotion of mutual support groups. For example, professional workers may move from helping individuals to helping groups of people develop their capacities to help each other (see Part 1, Chapter 2).

Alternatively, groups of people may come together on their own initiative to provide mutual support through common action and organisation as well as through individualised advice-giving or counselling (see Part 1, Chapter 2).

It is community if and when there is deliberate association between people: not association only in the sense of people being brought together, but the purposeful association which emerges when people themselves choose to come together; or having been brought together, choose to maintain contact with each other, to share concerns and work together and organise common actions.

A key element of this process is that people choose their own helping relationships and determine ultimately the shape and direction of the group activities which emerge.

Appendices

Appendix A

WHAT IS SOCIAL POLICY?

Social policy is discussed sometimes in terms of certain services provided by the state and local government, and sometimes in terms of other, different services provided by the state and local government. Sometimes it is discussed in terms of the purposes of the state and local government in seeking to bring about a different state of affairs in society or in seeking to change the lives of certain groups of people in society.

T.H. Marshall (1975) discussed social policy in terms of objectives of the state and local government in promoting the welfare of citizens by providing a core of services in social security, housing, community and health services and education.[1] Richard Titmuss (1974) saw social policy and social policy debates as being concerned about making choices between different objectives for changing society and about deciding what was 'the good society'.[2]

As discussed above, social policy represents intervention in people's lives. The state and local government intervene to provide services, and intervene by distributing or redistributing resources and by raising taxes to pay for services. They intervene also by seeking to regulate the behaviour of certain groups or individuals: for example, by regulating activities which may impinge on public health; or by requiring from adults, including parents, certain standards for the care of children.

Social policy may be presented simply as intervention to provide or offer help; but it may mean also intervention in people's lives for policing as well as helping purposes.[3] And particular social policies may be criticised for their perceived consequences. For example, Gillian Pascall (1986) believed that social policy played a key part in sustaining the dependence of women within families.[4] Although she acknowledged (1997) that subsequent developments in social policy had enhanced women's autonomy she argued that they had not removed the dependency of women within families.[5]

Ideas about what (some) people need, and the activities and services which should follow from such ideas, can lead to quite different conclusions about the role of the state and local government. Michael Walzer (1984) advocated the idea of political community and membership and what he saw as the mutual obligations of members. The first such obligation was the mutual provision of security and welfare.[6] Within his philosophy, in which the state and local government is part of the community, state action would seem a natural and logical consequence of there being a political community.

But conservative thinkers have taken a different view of social relations and obligations and the role of the state. For example, Roger Scruton (1991) emphasised association between people outside of government, referring to 'civil society' which he described as the totality of free associations. Mutual support could be provided by direct association and a multiplicity of associations.[7] This conservative idea of community could be taken to call into question the very idea of an active social policy by the state.

Commonly, social policy has been seen as something which the state and local government do: but the term 'social policy' can be applied to the objectives and activities of other bodies outside of the state and local government. Marilyn Taylor, Joan Langan and Paul Hoggett (1995) studied the diversity of organisations – large and small; charitable, local and private – which are engaged in community care services. They observed that these organisations emphasised such values as promoting independent living, facilitating mutual support between people with common experiences, working for the empowerment of the users of services. Such values became in effect, social policy objectives.[8]

Rudolf Klein and Jane Millar (1995) have articulated a view of social policy as a matter of individual enterprise, in which people make their own individual choices about the use of services which may be available in society: whether in housing, or pensions, or education, or health care.[9]

However social policy is interpreted or presented it expresses *values* about what is good or bad in society and it implies *choices* about what should be done. I would describe social policy as a body of ideas about how society is and how it ought to be, and what should be done to change it, and who should do it; or as a *different* body of ideas about how society is and how it ought to be and what then should be done to change it and who then should do it. Social policy means judgements about the situation of particular people or particular groups of people in society and what should or can be done to change their situations. Social policy judgements may lead to plans and systematic attempts to redistribute resources, including money in the form of benefits, or goods given directly to people who are considered to be in need of support. Social policy judgements may mean making available services, whether schools or houses or personal health care or transport. Social policy judgements may mean encouraging particular people or groups of people to do certain things; or imposing restraints on what other people can do.

But however it is described, social policy implies some idea of society and some sense of common concerns and common purposes between people in society.

REFERENCES

1. MARSHALL, T.H. (1975). *Social policy.* 4th. ed. London: Hutchinson. pp.11-12

2. TITMUSS, Richard. (1974). *Social policy.* London: Allen & Unwin. p.49

3. FERGÉ, Zsuzsa. (1994). Social policy, *Blackwell dictionary of 20th century social thought.* p.604

4. PASCALL, Gillian. (1986). *Social policy : a feminist analysis.* London: Tavistock. pp.28-29

5. PASCALL, Gillian. (1997). *Social policy : a new feminist analysis.* London: Routledge. p.25

6. WALZER, Michael. (1984). Membership, welfare and needs, *Liberalism and its critics.* Edited by Michael T. Sandel. Oxford: Blackwell. p.200

7. SCRUTON, Roger. (1991). Introduction: What is conservatism?, *Conservative texts*. p.10

8. HOGGETT, Paul, LANGAN, Joan, and TAYLOR, Marilyn. (1995). Encouraging diversity : voluntary and private organisations, *Community care*. Aldershot: Arena; Ashgate. pp.15-18

9. KLEIN, Rudolf, and MILLAR, Jane. (1995). Social policy : searching for a new paradigm?, *Social Policy and Administration* (Oxford: Blackwell). Vol.28, no.4 (December 1995). p.304

Appendix B

GLOSSARY OF CHEMICAL AND BIOLOGICAL TERMS AS USED IN CHAPTERS 4 AND 11

Element: Any substance that cannot be reduced to simpler substances by naturally occurring chemical processes: it is a fundamental substance.

It was in the 1660's that the English chemist Robert Boyle first described the elements in the terms in which they are understood today: as being primitive and simple, and not made from any other substances. Up to the present time, ninety-two chemical elements have been identified as occurring in nature, as distinct from elements which have been created artificially.

Hydrogen is by far the most abundant element in the universe. Of the elements composing the human body, or to which the human body can be reduced from cells and molecules, the most notable by weight are oxygen (65%), carbon (18%) and hydrogen (10%).

Carbon: An element which is fundamental to life. Compounds of carbon are described as 'organic' and organic chemistry is the study of carbon and its compounds. Over one million compounds of carbon are known. Carbon is present in all living matter.

Atom: The characteristics of the elements are the outcome, to a large degree, of the structure of their atoms.

The atom has been described by Stephen Hawking as the basic unit of matter (*A Brief History of Time*, p.201) and by Steven Rose as the smallest particle of an element (*The Chemistry of Life*, p.13). But the atom is not an elementary particle: it has an internal structure; it is built from smaller particles. The principal particles from which the atom is built are protons, neutrons and electrons. The protons and neutrons exist in the small central area or nucleus of the atom, where most of the mass is concentrated. The protons in the nucleus have a positive electric charge. They are balanced by negatively charged electrons which move around the nucleus of the atom.

There are always the same number of protons as electrons in the atom of a given element. At one end of the range of the elements, the hydrogen atom has one proton and one electron. At the other end of the range the uranium atom consists of ninety-two protons and ninety-two electrons.

Molecule: Any group of atoms bonded together so that they act as a unit. When atoms approach one another closely, the electrons of each atom may interact with the electrons of another atom so intensely as to bond together and form a molecule.

Molecules may be simple and small or complex and large. Macromolecules contain at least one thousand atoms each. The more complex molecules have developed over time (an awful lot of time!) from simple beginnings in the early primitive earth.

Organic molecules are molecules containing carbon (see above). Complex molecules such as amino acids, the building blocks of the giant protein molecules (see below), or nucleotides, from which are built the nucleic acid molecules such as DNA (see below) may have formed in the early primitive atmosphere of Earth when there was a combination of limited free oxygen and a strong energy source. That energy source could have been provided by lightning, or ultraviolet radiation, or kinetic energy – the energy derived from the motion of bodies such as the impact on earth of incoming meteorites. This possibility has been confirmed by laboratory experiments in which enclosed gas mixtures of hydrogen, methane and ammonia were subjected to prolonged electric charge and produced eventually various complex organic molecules. It is this type of complex organic molecule which helps to constitute organisms which exist at the present time.

It has been argued that some of the complex organic molecules may have been imported to Earth 4 to 3.8 billion years ago. The existence of such molecules beyond Earth has been confirmed by probes sent from Earth to investigate Halley's Comet and Titan, one of the moons of Saturn (see *Book of Life*, p.38)

Life: A great deal is known about life, but there is not general agreement about what life is. Daniel E. Koshland Jr. recalled a scientific conference at which many hours of discussion on the question: 'What is the definition of life?' could not resolve the question. It seemed that everyone knew what life was but could not agree on a definition of it (*Science*, 2002).

One reason may be that it is difficult to draw a hard and fast dividing line between the living and the non-living. Clearly some things are living and some things are not living. The living and the non-living are connected to each other; but the connection is subtle and long drawn out.

From an evolutionary perspective, all organisms on Earth have come from other, earlier organisms. But this means that the first life forms on Earth must have come from non-living matter. This is not so difficult to imagine if it is realised that matter is not still. Matter is in a constant state of movement and change because the atoms and molecules which constitute matter are in a constant state of interaction and development.

The primitive Earth's atmosphere was composed of gases which would be poisonous to present day organisms. But over time (an awful lot of time) substances, compounds and – later – life forms developed which made room for themselves and adapted the atmosphere to be what we know today.

Life forms may have emerged either from single molecules with an ability to replicate, to make copies of themselves; or from the coming together of networks and structures of reacting/interacting molecules which were capable of making copies of themselves, of reproducing.

DNA (Deoxyribonucleic Acid): A giant nucleic acid molecule (and the largest known molecule) which carries the blueprint for the design and assembly of protein molecules, which are the basic building blocks of life and of organisms, including human beings. The DNA molecule may be considered as a guide book for building an organism – whether it be a plant or insect or animal or a human being. The structure of the DNA molecule follows the shape of a coiled doubled helix, like a spiral staircase with two strands. Each strand has a series of bases arranged horizontally, and each is attached to a complementary base from the other strand: like the succeeding steps on a spiral staircase, or the rungs on a ladder.

The bases are the part of the DNA molecule which varies. It is the precise sequence of the bases, the pattern in the way in which they vary, which carries the information which can be used as sets of instructions. A set of three bases provides the code for the assembly of each of the twenty amino acids which are the building blocks of the protein molecule. Which set of bases provides the code for which amino acid adds up to the 'genetic code'.

The genetic code appears to be universal in all forms of life from bacteria to human beings. The same sets of bases of the DNA molecule provide the code for the same amino acids, whatever the life form.

Gene: A functional segment of DNA. It carries a body of information which can be used as a set of instructions for the design and assembly of a protein molecule. It can be said to encode for a protein molecule.

Like the majority of actors, DNA and genes tend to work only occasionally. To begin with, most DNA does not encode for protein molecules. Most DNA simply 'hangs around' doing nothing in particular. Furthermore the protein molecule is encoded by a relatively small part of a gene (*Biodiversity*. p.282). And, like actors, genes tend to respond if and when roles are offered. When the product of a particular gene is needed, the segment of the DNA molecule containing that gene will split, and a segment of the RNA molecule will be formed and will attach itself to the segment of the DNA molecule, and then facilitate the building of a protein molecule from the information which the gene provides.

A gene may be described as a unit of information as to how some things can be done. In a longer perspective, beyond encoding for a particular protein molecule, it can be said that the function of a gene is determined by the way the cell (see below) which houses the DNA in its nucleus, is able to make use, for its own growth and development, of the information which the gene encodes.

Genes may be considered as units of heredity in that each organism's genes contain information which can be used to build its offspring. They constitute sets of messages which are passed on by an elaborate process from one generation to the next through special cells called 'gametes' (see below).

RNA (Ribonucleic Acid): A giant nucleic acid molecule, similar to DNA which acts as an intermediary, extracting the information from DNA which is required for building protein molecules.

Protein: A giant molecule, built from smaller molecules, the amino acids. Protein molecules are the basic building blocks of life. They are present in all living matter. There are thousands of different kinds of protein molecules.

Enzyme: A form of protein; the working molecule of life; a catalyst for biochemical reactions in organisms, including human beings: for example, degrading food into smaller molecules for digestion. There is a specific enzyme for each biochemical reaction.

There are hundreds of enzymes in a cell. They create new chemical structures for cells as the cells grow and develop.

Cells: The smallest unit of which living tissues and organs are composed. Cells are like compartments with dividing walls or membranes. They are miniature biochemical factories: under the microscope they demonstrate intense activity. All life is composed of cells and all the major changes that occur in plants and animals and human beings came about as the result of changes in the properties of numerous cells. Throughout our lives the cells of our bodies are dividing constantly.

Some of the earliest or simplest life forms such as bacteria consist of only one cell. In a single cell life form, the cells are very versatile. As more and more complex life forms develop, each with more and more cells, the individual cells become more specialised and less versatile. The evolution of specialised cells is responsible for the great diversity of life forms.

There are two main types of cell. The simpler, more primitive prokaryotic cell is characteristic of simpler organisms such as bacteria. The more complex eukaryotic cell is characteristic of plants, animals and human beings. Eukaryotic cells have a nucleus which contains the genetic material of DNA in chromosomes.

Prokaryotic cells evolved first. Fossil records suggest that they evolved around or by three thousand million years ago. It is not known when eukaryotic cells began to evolve, except that it was most likely to have been between three hundred and fifty million and seven hundred million years ago.

Chromosomes: A long strand of DNA: the molecular structure which packages the genes. A gene has a fixed position on a chromosome.

It is through chromosomes that genes and the information they hold are passed from existing cells to new cells. This happens because throughout our lives the cells in our bodies are dividing constantly (*see above*). For a cell to divide, each chromosome will divide into identical halves so that each new cell contains the same number of chromosomes as the parent cell.

Genes and the information they hold are also passed from existing cells to new cells when cells fuse in the process of sexual reproduction. The cells which fuse are special cells called gametes (eggs in the female; sperm in the male, which contain a single set of chromosomes. Through these cells, each parent provides half of the chromosomes of their offspring, so that their offspring each have the same number of chromosomes as each of their parents.

SOURCES

Concise science dictionary. (1991). 2nd ed. Oxford: Oxford University Press.

Encyclopedia Britannica. (1994). 15th ed. Micropedia. Vols.3, 4, 5, 6

Encyclopedia Britannica. (1994). 15th ed. Macropedia. Vol.22

GOULD, Stephen Jay (ed.). (1993). *The Book of Life*. London: Ebury Hutchinson

GREENSPAN, Ralph J. (1995). Understanding the genetic construction of behaviour, *Scientific American* (New York: Scientific American Inc.). Vol.272, no.4 (April 1995). pp.72-78

HAWKING, Stephen. (1995). *A brief history of time*. London: Bantam

KITCHER, Philip. (1996). *The lives to come : the genetic revolution and human possibilities*. London: Allen Lane / Penguin.

KOSHLAND, Daniel E. Jr. (2002). The seven pillars of life, *Science* (Washington: AAAS). Vol. 295 (22 March 2002). pp.2215-2216

MARKS, Jonathan. (1995). *Bio-diversity : genes, race and history.* New York: Aldine de Gruyter.

MEDAWAR, P.B., and MEDAWAR, J.S. (1984). *Aristotle to zoos : a philosophical dictionary of biology*. London: Weidenfeld & Nicolson

PURVES, William ... [et al]. (1998). *Life : the science of biology*. 5th ed. Sunderland, MS: Sinauer.

RIDLEY, Mark. (1985). *The Problems of evolution.* Oxford: Oxford University Press.

ROSE, Steven. (1991). *The Chemistry of Life*. 3rd ed. Harmondsworth: Penguin.

INDEX

Abrams, Philip, 72-73, 108, 116, 158
Accountability, 179
Africa, 67
Afro-Caribbeans, 27, 105
Ageing
  See: Elderly persons
Agriculture
  See: Farming
Ahmad, Waqar I.U, 109
Aid programmes, 2
AIDS, 109
Alcohol abuse, 35
Allan, Graham, 92, 133, 144, 150
Allan, Shula, 27
Altruism and altruistic behaviour, 54-56, 64-66, 70-72, 74-77
Ancient human communities, 71-72
Archaeology, 120
Armagh County (Northern Ireland), 45
Archer, Colin, 31
Area Regeneration Programmes, 38-48, 173-175, 178, 180-181
Areas of special need, 39, 41
Ark Housing Project, 142
Asians, 105, 109
Asimov, Isaac, 169
Associations, forms of, 2, 6, 7, 8, 52, 54, 74-75, 89, 94, 139, 174
  See *also:* Networks
    Social networks
Atema, Jelle, 161
Atkin, Karl, 103, 104, 105, 106, 107
Atoms, 80, 195
Audit Commission for England and Wales, 17
Austria, 155-157
Axelrod, Robert, 55, 65
Bacteria, 68-70
  see also Myxococcus xanthus
    rhizobium
Balfour, Arthur James, 42, 119
Banks and banking, 121
  See also: Capitalism
    Globalisation
    Trade and commerce
Bangladesh, 93, 150, 154, 183
Baptista, Luis, 161
Barber, Benjamin, 151
Barclay, Peter
  see Barclay Report ...
Barclay Report on the Future of Social Work, 4, 20, 90, 103
Barkow, Jerome H, 56
Barr, Alan, 103
Barry, Nicola, 31
Bartlett, Robert, 121
Batley, Richard, 38
Beaumont, Justin, 43
Beckett, J.C, 47
Belfast, 33
Belfast Action Teams, 34, 38, 41, 178
Belfast Areas of Need, 38
Belfast Work Strategy
Bell, Colin, 141
Berger, Peter, 148
Berlin, Isaiah, 134-135
Bernera (of Lewis), 93
Bernstein, Andrea, 96-97
Berry, Christopher, 151
Berthaud, R, 11
Biological change, 56-57, 59, 61
Biological determinism, 55
  See also: Genetic determinism
    Social determinism
Biological processes, 55-58
Biology, 195-201
Birmingham, 27
Birrell, Derek, 42
Black, Antony, 121

Black Sea, 120
Blackwell Dictionary of 20th Century Social Thought, 90
Bloom, Paul, 169
Bluebond-Langner, M, 157
Boddy, Martin, 116
Boesch, Christopher, 67
Booth, Tim, 24-25
Booth, Wendy, 24-25
Bornat, I, 114
Bouchard, Thomas J, 62-63, 162
Bowler, Peter J, 61
Boyle, Robert, 195
Bradley, Carmel, 45
Briggs, Anna, 21, 105
British National Party (BNP), 136
Brompton, Kevin, 109
Brown, Hilary, 18, 168, 175
Broxtowe Better Way to Health Group, 33
Buber, Martin, 88, 183
Bulmer, Martin, 5, 72, 108, 111, 116, 158
Burns, J.H, 130, 166
Bystander intervention, 75

California, 92
Canada, 125
See also: North America
United States ...
Capitalism, 121
See also: Banks and banking
Globalisation
Trade and commerce
Caplan, Arthur L, 81
Carbon, 195
Care and caring
See also: Reciprocal care
Care in the community
see Community care
Care in the Community Demostration Programme, 16
Carers, 35, 104-113
See also: Charitable organisations
Carers (contd)
See also: Informal care
Voluntary organisations
Carers' National Association, 105, 106
Castells, Manuel, 116
Cecil, Rosanne, 21, 110
Cells, 56-57, 199
Cesarani, David, 136
Charitable organisations, 17
See also: Informal care
Voluntary organisations
Chemistry, 195-201
Cheshire Sexual Abuse Support Line, 31
Cheshire Social Services Dept, 31
Children and illness, 157
Children and Young Persons Act 1963 (GB)
Children and Young Persons Act 1969 (GB)
Chimpanzees, 67, 71
Choice, 73-74, 79, 148, 156, 163, 176, 192
Chromosomes, 200
City and cities
See also: Urban...
City Challenge Programme, 39, 40, 41-42
City Action Teams, 39
Civil society, 71, 192
Clarke, Gordon L, 124
Cohen, Anthony, 133, 146, 168
Cohen, Michael D, 65
Cohen, Stanley, 143, 157
Coleman, Janet, 121
Communication, 67-68, 94, 179
See also: Mass media
Transport
Communism
See: Marx, Karl

Community
 See: Ancient human
 Communities
 Community and belonging
 Community and place
 Community as a metaphor
 Community care
 Community profiles
 Community, integration in
 Community, rehabilitation
 Community, relocation ...
 International communities
 Limited applicability,
 community as an ...
 Local communities
 Political community
 Therapeutic communities
 Unitary communities
 Unitary idea of community
 Victorian vision of ...
Community and belonging, 141-144, 145-170
Community and locality
 See: Community and place
Community and place, 88-98, 119, 174-176
Community as a metaphor, 177-178
Community care, 2, 4, 5, 15-23, 24, 27, 103-114, 175, 180, 192
 See also: Griffiths Report
Community Development Foundation, 33
Community Development Review Group (Northern Ireland), 135-136
Community, integration in the, 25-26, 28, 29-30, 159, 173
Community nursing services, 90, 175
Community of limited liability, 111
Community profiles, 3
Community, rehabiliation in the, 173
Community, relocation in the, 4
Community Support Programme (Northern Ireland), 35, 158
Comte, Auguste, 117
Competition and competitiveness, 64, 79
Conflicts of values, 74, 132-137, 163
Congested Districts Boards (Ireland), 42-43
Conscience, 154
Consciousness, 147, 148, 149, 163
Co-operation and co-operative behaviour, 6, 52, 54-56, 64-72, 76-77, 79, 88, 119
Cornwell, Jocelyn, 92, 135
Cosmides, Leda, 67
Coveney, Peter, 66
Cox, Kevin R, 131
Craigintinney Health Project, Edinburgh, 37, 143
Crain, Stephen, 160
Crow, Graham, 92, 133, 144, 150
Culture and cultural traditions, 67. 75, 94, 96, 151, 153
Cumberledge, Julia
 See: Cumberledge Report ...
Cumberledge Report on
Community Nursing Services in England and Wales, 90, 175

Dalley, Gillian, 5, 25
Darwin, Charles, 58-59
Dawkins, Richard, 162
Day care services, 17
Day, Graham, 45, 91, 150, 154, 182
Daz, Dr, 20
Deaf people, 35
Deakin, Nicholas, 39
Decision making, 73
Definition, problems of, 9, 97
Denmark, 63

Deoxyribonucleic acid (DNA), 57-58, 197-198
Dependency, 104-114
De Scola, Philippe, 119
Determinism
See: Biological determinism
Genetic determinism
Sociological determinism
Diasporas
See: International communities
Disability, 4, 19, 28, 29-30, 31, 35, 90-91, 104, 173
See also: Lothian Disabled People's ...
Mental handicap
Mental illness
Disease, genetic influences in, 63
DNA
see Deoxyribonucleic acid
Domicilary services, 17
Donne, John, 51
Donnison, David, 150
Drug abuse, 35
Drysdale, Jack, 103
Dumfries and Galloway Mental Health Association, 32
Dunning, John H, 125
Durban (South Africa), 96-97
Dyson, Freeman, 165

Economic change, 115-131
Economic conditions, 3, 7
Eddington, Arthur Stanley, 115
Edinburgh, 19, 27, 37, 143
Edinburgh Association for Mental Health, 27
Education Priority Areas Programme, 38-39, 41
Edwards, John, 38, 39
Eichmann, Adolf, 156
Elderly persons, 20, 24, 26, 104, 107, 108, 110
Elements, 195
Emerson, Eric, 4, 25-26, 90
Empathy, 76
Employment and carers, 104-105
Engels, Friedrich, 167
England, 4, 20, 24, 38, 90, 103
Enterprise zones, 39
Environment, Dept. of (GB), 40, 42
Enzymes, 199
Equal Opportunities Commission (Northern Ireland), 104, 112
Ethnic minorities
See: Minority ethnic groups
Ethnography, 119
Europe (Medieval), 120-122
European Commission, 43
European Community, 38
Evason, Eileen, 104, 105, 106
Evolution, 55, 58-61, 64-71, 162, 197
Exeter, 108
Existence
See: Unique existence

Fabricius, Ida, 116
Fagan, Brian M, 120
Family centres, 33-34
Family relationships, 21, 29, 104-113, 117-118, 120, 122-123, 126-127
see also Marriage
Farge, James K, 130
Farming, 91
See also: Rural society
Fehr, Ernst, 65
Feminism, 5
see also Women
Fergé, Zsuysa, 193
Feynman, Richard, 164-165
Finland, 63
Fischer, Claude S, 126
Fisher, Mike, 106, 107, 109
Forms of association
see Association, forms of
Foster, R.F, 48
Free will
See: Choice

Freedom
See: Human liberty

Gächter, Simon, 65
Gallese, Vittorio, 76
Games theory, 66, 75
Gandhi Hall, Manchester, 19-20, 26
Gardner, Katy, 93, 150, 154, 183
GEAR Project (Glasgow), 150-151
Gemeinschaft, 117
General Household Survey (GB), 105
General Improvement Areas, 38
General Social Survey (USA), 126
Genes and genetics, 56-58, 60-63, 73, 161-162, 164, 177, 198-199
see also Selfish genes
Genetic determinism, 162, 163
Geras, Norman, 154
Gergen, Kenneth J, 168
Germany, 156
Gert, Bernard, 81
Gertier, Meric S, 125
Gesellschaft, 117
Gibson, Michael, 43, 45-46
Giddens, Anthony, 120-121, 122, 151, 152
Gilbert, Walter, 57-58, 162
Gilligan, Robbie, 16
Glasgow, 150-151
Glendinning, Caroline, 104
Globalisation, 115-116, 124-126
Goffman, Irving, 151
Goldman, Alvin, 76
Gould, Stephen Jay, 64
Government policy, 3, 15, 103, 191-194
Gray, Marilyn, 96-97
Gray, Patricia M, 161
Green, Karen, 54
Greenberg, Joseph, 160
Greenspan, Ralph J, 62-63
Gribbin, John, 165
Gribbin, Mary, 165
Griffiths, Jonathan, 29-30
Griffiths Report, 17, 18, 175
Griffiths, Roy
See: Griffiths Report
Group homes, 18, 19, 28
Group work practice, 30-36
Groups, 9, 30-36, 186
Guilds and fraternities, 122
Gulf War, 126-127

Haffenden, Sharon, 104
Haifa, 127
Hambleton, Robin, 134
Hamilton, William D, 65
Hamnett, Chris, 43, 99
Handsworth Community Care Centre, Birmingham, 27
Hardy, Henry, 137
Harris, Nigel, 116
Harris, Rosemary, 91, 153
Hatton, Chris, 4, 25-26, 90
Hawking, Stephen, 195
Health, 92
See also: Disability
Disease
Illness
Health and Social Services, Dept. of (Northern Ireland), 17
Health care, 24-37
Health education, 33
Health, Dept. of (GB), 15-16, 19, 20
Health, Minister of (GB), 11
Health services, 16, 17, 24
Helping relationships, 180, 186, 187
Henderson, Paul, 103
Henwood, Melanie, 106
Herbert, David T, 48
Heredity, 58-61
Hewitt, John, 139
Hicks, Cherrill, 109
Highfield, Roger, 66
Hill, Malcolm, 46

Hinshelwood, R.D, 37
Hirst, Paul, 124
Hitler, Adolf, 156
Hobbes, Thomas, 53-54, 64
Hobson, Vicki, 32, 143
Hoggett, Paul, 192
Holocaust, the, 75
Holzhausen, Emily, 105
Home Office (GB), 59
Hondagneu-Sotelo, Pierrette, 92
Hoo, Leroy, 82, 169
Hospitals, relocation from, 4, 15, 24-26, 90-91
Hostels, 24
House of Commons Social Services Committee, 19, 175
Housing, 38-39
Housing Action Areas, 38-39
Housing Action Trusts, 40
Housing redevelopment, 141
Hughes, Geraint, 3
Human Genome Project, 57-58
Human liberty, 53-54, 159
Human rights, 53-54
Hunt, Albert, 5
Hunt, Audrey, 105
Hunter, A.H, 111
Hunter, David, 17
Hunter, James, 48
Hunter-gatherers, 71-72
Hybridisation, 59-61
Hydrogen, 195

Identity, sense of, 93, 164, 176
Illness, 92, 108
See also: Health
Disease
Immigrant workers, 92
Independent living, 25, 177
Indian people, 20, 26
Individualism and individualist behaviour, 6, 52-56, 72, 88, 148-149, 152, 160, 164
Industrial Revolution, 117
Industrial society, 7, 115
Industrialisation, 123
Informal care, 15-23, 107, 110
See also: Carers
Charitable organisations
Voluntary organisations
Inner city areas, 39
Institutional care, 18, 24, 175
Inter-Departmental Committee on Rural Development (Northern Ireland), 40
International communities, 94-95
International Encyclopaedia of the Social Sciences, 148
International migration, 150, 154
Ireland (pre-1921), 42-43
Ireland, Republic of, 16
Iron Age, 120
Israel, 126-127
See also: Jews
Ithon Valley (Wales), 45, 91, 150, 182

Jaggerstatter, Franz, 155-157
James, Alison, 157
James, William, 160
Janowitz, M, 111
Jews, 75, 154-155
See also: Israel
Jones, Helen, 47
Jones, Maxwell, 30-31

Kaiser, Dale, 69, 78
Kevles, Daniel J, 82, 169
Keynes, John Maynard, 64
Kilmurray, Avila, 45
Kinship
see Family relationships
Reciprocity
Kirklees Relocation Project, 24
Kitcher, Philip, 63, 161
Klein, Rudolf, 192
Knox, Paul, 43, 131
Koresh, Yael, 126
Koshland, Daniel E. Jr., 197
Krause, Bernie, 161

Kroos, Lee, 69, 78
Krumhansl, Carol, 161
Kuper, Adam, 67-68, 71, 129

La Gory, Mark, 95-96
Lambert, Christine, 116
Lambeth (London), 43
Land rights, 121
Langan, Joan, 192
Langstaff, Michael, 43, 45-46, 141
Language and language use, 67-68, 76-77, 160-161, 177
Lansley, John, 47
Lawson, Dot, 105
Learning difficulties, 4, 25, 90-91, 142
Leeds, 45-46, 141
Lenski, Richard, 69, 78
Lichtenstein, Paul, 84
Ligoniel Family Centre, 33-34
Limited applicability, community as an idea of, 180-181
Liverpool, 45-46, 141
Local authority care, 17, 24
Local authorities, 134
Local community, 2-3, 7, 19, 40-41, 44, 89-90, 93, 97, 149, 178
Local government policy, 191-194
London, 43, 92, 135
London, hospitals, 30-31
Long, Norton E, 80, 152
Loomis, Charles P, 129
Losick, Richard, 69, 78
Lothian Disabled People's Coalition, 31
Lothian Health Board, 143
Lucknow, Thomas, 148
Lynch, Bruce, 4, 16, 36
Lynch, Felix, 19

MacAulay, Donald, 93
MacAmhlaigh, Domhnall
see MacAulay, Donald
MacDonnell, L, 99
Machiavelli, Niccolo, 134-135
Making Belfast Work, 38, 40, 42, 44, 90, 178
Malcolm, Marion, 142
Mamitora, Mr., 20
Manchester, 20, 40
Manhattan Project, 164
Manning, N, 37
Marks, Jonathan, 163
Marriage, 122-123
see also Family relationships
Marshall, T. H, 191
Marx, Karl, 64, 152-153
Mass media, 115
Maudsley Hospital, London, 30-31
May, Robert, 68
McGregor, Suzanne, 39
McKnight, John L, 18, 19, 28, 175
McLellan, David, 167
McShane, Liz, 35, 158
Medawar, J.S, 83
Medawar, P.B, 83
Medieval Europe, 117, 118, 120-123, 148
Medieval society, 117, 120-123
See also: Older societies
Mendel, Gregor, 59-61
Mental handicap, 15
Mental health, 27, 32, 142
Mental Health Act 1959 (GB), 17
Mental illness, 15, 27, 32
See also: Royal Commission ...
Schizophrenia
Mexicans, 92
Middle ages
see Medieval ...
Middleton, Alan, 150
Midgley, Mary, 74, 76, 133, 159, 160
Migration, 92-94, 115, 122, 183
See also: Immigrant workers
International migration

Migration (contd)
See also: Population movement
Millar, Jane, 192
Mind reading, 76-77
Minimal state, the, 54
Minnesota, University of, Centre for Twin and Adoption Research, 62
Minority ethnic groups, 94, 108
see also Afro-Caribbeans
Asians
Indians
Mexicans
Mirror neurons, 76
Mischel, Theodore, 168
Modern societies *cf.* older societies, 117, 118-123
Molecules, 57-58, 196
Mollenkopf, John H, 116-117
Morris, B, 27
Morris, Jenny, 28, 158
Motivation, 74-75
Mulvey, Lami, 32, 143
Murdoch, Jonathan, 45, 91, 150
Music, 161, 177, 182
Musselburgh (Scotland), 142
Myxococcus xanthus, 69, 78

National Health Service, 107
National Health Service and Community Care Act 1990 (GB), 15
Natural selection, 59, 61, 70, 71
Nazis and nazism, 154-155
Neal, L, 124
Neighbours and neighbouring, 110, 111, 119, 136, 153-154, 182-183
See also: Abrams, Philip
Networks, 4, 20, 91, 92, 119, 120, 143
See *also:* Associations
Social networks
Neurons, 76
see also Mirror neurons
New England, 18, 19, 28
Newby, Howard, 141
Newton, Isaac, 164
New York, 116-117
Newry and Mourne Carers' Association, 35
Nisbet, Robert, 117, 120, 133
Non-institutional services, 18
Normalisation, 25
North America, 120
See also: Canada
United States ...
Northern Ireland, 20, 35, 38, 40, 91, 104, 105, 110, 135-136, 139, 153, 158
Northern Ireland Deaf Youth Association, 35
Northern Ireland Housing Executive, 34
Nottingham, 33
Nowak, Martin, 68
Nozick, Robert, 1, 6, 54, 77, 89, 141, 164
Nursing services, 90
See also: Home nursing

Oasis Project, Edinburgh, 27
O'Connor, Kevin, 124
Offer, John, 21, 110
Old persons and older persons
See: Elderly persons
Older societies
See also: Ancient human communities,
Iron Age,
Palaeo-Indians,
Pre-literate societies
Older societies (contd)
See also: Traditional societies
Older societies *cf.* modern societies, 117, 118-123
Oliver, Judith, 21, 105
Ontario, 125
Oppenheimer, Robert, 165
Original solitude, 77-78, 88
Out of House Project, 143

Oxford English Dictionary, 1-2

P.A. Cambridge Economic Consultants, 46-47
Pahl, Raymond, 141
Palaeo-Indians, 120
PANDA (People's Alternative to Drug and Alcohol abuse, 35
Park, Robert E, 152
Participation, 179
Parker, Gillian, 15, 18, 104, 105
Pascall, Gillian, 34-35, 191
Payne, Roger, 161
Pearlman, Vicky, 105
Penrose, Roger, 165
Percy-Smith, Jaine, 3
Perry, Richard, 4, 16, 36
Personal help, 7
Personal relationships, 180
Personal social services, 20
See also: Seebohm Report ...
Personal Social Services Research Unit (PSSRU), 15
Pervis, Laurence A
Petch, Alison, 142, 158
Philosophy
See: Political philosophy
Philpott, Terry, 11
Physics, 164-165
Pinker, Robert, 5
Pinker, Steven, 61-62, 160-161, 163
Pipkin, John, 95-96
Pisan, Christine de, 81
Pipkin, John, 95-96
Plant, Raymond, 52, 115, 138, 181
Pleistocene period, 70
Police officers, 110
Poltical community, 192
Political philosophy, 134-135
Popper, Karl, 9, 74, 132
Population growth, 121
Population movement, 121, 124, 127
See also: Migration
Poverty, 2, 38-48
Pre-literate societies, 119
See also: Ancient human communities,
Older societies
Traditional societies
Primatology, 67, 71
Prisoner's Dilemma, 66
Proteins, 199
Punishment, 65

Quakers, 29
Quillet, Jeannine, 121, 148

Race, 163
Racial inequality, 105
Racism, 136
Raistrick, Jane, 137
Ramachandran, V.S, 76-77
Rapport, Nigel, 168
Reciprocal care, 116
Reciprocity, 73
Redevelopment, 46
Rehabilitation
See: Community, rehabilation ..
Relationships
See: Helping relationships
Personal relationships
Social relationships
Religious divisions, 153-154
Relocation
See: Community, relocation .. .
Hospitals, relocation ...
Kirklees Relocation Project
Reproduction, 56-57
Rescuers, 154-155
Residential care, 28
Residential institutions, 158
Residential services, 17
Reynolds, Susan, 121, 122
Rhizobium, 69
Ribonucleic acid (RNA), 199
Ridley, Mark, 61
Ridley, Matt, 64, 65-66, 70, 72, 77, 80, 120

Rigel, Stephnie, 5
Riolo, Rick L, 65
RNA
 see Ribonucleic acid
Rollings, Janet, 105
Roman Catholic Church, 155-156
Rorty, Richard, 168
Rose, Steven, 57, 195
Rosenberg, Nancy, 148, 151
Rothman, Barbara Katz, 80
Royal Commission on the Law Relating to Mental Illness, 15
Royal Edinburgh Hospital, 27
Rural Challenge, 40
Rural development, 38-48
Rural Development Programmes, 40
Rural society, 122
 See also: Farming

Sandel, Michael T, 193
Sarré, P, 99
Savage, Mike, 96
Scales, John, 9
Schizophrenia, 32
 See also: Mental illness
Schwartz, Barry, 75
Scientific enquiry, 9, 164, 165
Scotland, 142, 158
Scruton, Roger, 192
Seebohm Report on the Personal Social Services in England and Wales, 4, 20, 38, 39, 90, 103
Self-help, 2, 179
Self-help groups, 32-36, 158
Selfhood, 145-170, 164
 See also: Social construction of self,
  Social sense of self
Self-interest, 6, 7, 54, 64-66, 71, 72-74, 80, 116
Selfish genes, 73
Service, Robert W, 141
Sexual abuse, 31
Shavit, Yossi, 126
Sheehan, Michael M, 122-123
Sheltered accommodation
 See: Supported accommodation
Sheppey, Isle of (London), 141
Sibley, David, 148
Sickness
 See: AIDS
  Disease
  Illness
Sigmund, Karl, 68
Simic, Paul, 27
Simon Resettlement Scheme (Larne), 158
Simons, Ken, 24-25
Single Regeneration Budget, 40
Slavery, 133
Smith, David M, 48
Smith, Helen, 18, 168, 175
Smith, John Maynard, 77
Smith, Michael Peter, 127
Smith, Randal, 137
Snare, Dawn, 116
Snieder, Roel, 9
Social audits, 3
Social behaviour, 52-53
Social change, 115-131
Social construction of self, 149-159
Social contact, 175
Social deprivation, 41
Social determinism, 75, 162, 163
 See also: Biological determinism
Social exclusion, 2, 135, 138-140
Social inclusion, 135, 138-140
Social networks, 126-127, 183
Social pathology, 39
Social policy, 2, 5, 7, 10, 173-174, 184-187, 191-194
Social policy as intervention, 191
Social relationships, 4, 6, 19, 28-29, 117, 138-139, 175-176, 181-182, 187
Social sense of self, 153, 157, 176-177

Social services, 17, 24
Social work & social workers, 4, 20, 24-37, 110
See also: Barclay Report ...
see also Biological determinism
South Africa, 96-97
Special aid programmes
see Area Regeneration Programmes
Species, origin of, 58, 83
St. Leger, Fred, 21, 110
Stoke Newington (London), 92
Support activities, 90, 96-97, 108-110
Support services, 103-104
Supported accommodation, 18, 142, 158
See also: Sheltered accommodation
Suttles, Gerald D, 90, 111
Sweden, 63
Swindon, 116
Sylhet (Bangladesh), 93, 150, 154
Szivas, Sue, 25

Taylor, Laurie, 143, 157
Taylor, Marilyn, 192
Taylor, Peter J, 131
Technologies, new, 116
Therapeutic communities, 30-32, 173
Thompson, Grahame, 124
Titterton, Michael, 168
Titmuss, Richard, 191
Tönnies, Ferdinand, 117-118
Tooby, John, 67
Tower Hamlets (London), 136
Townsend, Peter, 43
Trade and commerce, 96-97, 120, 121, 124-125
See also: Banks and banking, Capitalism Globalisation
Traditional societies, 111
See also: Ancient human communities, Older societies, Pre-literate societies
Trafford Park Urban Development Corporation, 40
Transport, 94
Trinity Centre, Edinburgh, 19
Trivers, Robert L, 65, 70
Twigg, Julia, 103, 104, 106, 107
Twins, 62-63, 162-163
Tyne, Alan, 29, 158

Ukraine, 120
Unemployment, 38
Unique existence, 164, 166
Unitary communities, 10, 45
Unitary idea of community, 173-174, 178
United Kingdom, 4, 26, 103, 124-125, 134
United Nations Research Institute for Social Development, 115, 116
United States of America, 18, 19, 28, 80, 90, 92, 126, 134, 137, 152
See also: Canada North America
UNRISD
See: United Nations Research Institute for Social Development
Urban Development Corporations 39
Urban government, 134
See also: Local authorities
Urban growth, 121
Urban life, 80, 96, 117, 151-152
Urban Programme, 38, 39, 41
Urban redevelopment, 38-48
Urban renewal, 141
Urban society, 115
Urban Task Forces, 39, 40

Urbanisation, 115, 117, 121-124, 126
Urbanism, 118
URBEX Project, 43, 48

Values, 74, 132-137, 147, 192
Velicer, Gregory, 69, 78
Victorian vision of community, 119
Violence, 159
Voluntary organisations, 16, 21
See also: Carers
Charitable organisations
Informal care
Von Gierke, Otto, 117

Wales, 4, 20, 24, 38, 45, 91, 103, 106, 154, 182
Walker, Alan, 11, 15
Walzer, Michael, 192
War
See: Gulf War
World War II
Ward, Linda, 25
Warde, Alan, 96
Warner, Alan, 140
Warren, Roland, 133-134
Watson, James, 58
Waves, 9
Weddle, Ian, 31-32
Welfare policy, 15
Wenger, Clare, 106, 107, 108, 109
Western Isles (Scotland), 93
Whales, 161
Whitely, Stuart, 32
Whiten, Andrew, 67
Whittington, Dorothy, 104, 105, 106
Williams, Raymond, 98, 133, 147
Willmott, Peter, 95-96, 182-183
Wilson, Carol, 42
Wilson, Edward, 61, 65, 73
Wilson, Elizabeth, 5
Wilson, Melda, 31
Wilson, Thomas C, 126, 167
Wirth, Louis, 118, 152
Wistow, Gerard, 17
Women
See also: Feminism
Women and community, 45, 92
Women and violence, 29, 159
Women, as carers, 5, 21, 104
Women as dependants, 191
Women in the philosophy of Thomas Hobbes, 54, 71
Women traders, 96-97
Women workers, 92
Women's aid refuges, 34-35
Women's groups, 33-34
Women's health, 143
Woollacott, Martin, 94-95
Wordsworth, William, 164
World War II, 30-31
Wright, R, 92

Zahn, Gordon, 155-157
Zipf, George Kingsley, 95